Biblical Roads
to
Financial
Freedom

Biblical Roads
to
Financial
Freedom

Robert W. Katz CPA
with Jamie Katz

Treasure House

An Imprint of
Destiny Image® Publishers, Inc.
P.O. Box 310
Shippensburg, PA 17257-0310

"For where your treasure is, there will your heart be also."
Matthew 6:21

ISBN 0-7684-3015-1

For Worldwide Distribution
Printed in the U.S.A.

1 2 3 4 5 6 7 8 9 10 / 09 08 07 06 05 04 30

This book and all other Destiny Image, Revival Press, MercyPlace, Fresh Bread, Destiny Image Fiction, and Treasure House books are available at Christian bookstores and distributors worldwide.

For a U.S. bookstore nearest you, call
1-800-722-6774.
For more information on foreign distributors, call
717-532-3040.
Or reach us on the Internet:
www.destinyimage.com

DEDICATION

Of one blessing I am sure—my wife. I often stand in amazement at how the Lord works in her. She is an incredibly loving wife, a gifted and loving mother to our children, a bold teacher and student of the Word, and a passionate pursuer of the Lord. This book and most of the things that have value in my life would not be, but for Jamie. I love you and dedicate this book to you.

Acknowledgments

I never write alone; rather I try to follow the leading of the Holy Spirit and build upon the wisdom of those who have cared enough to disciple me.

No man has had a more profound influence on my life than my pastor, Michael Millé. You have poured into my life more scriptural wisdom, godly integrity, and passion for the eternal than I ever imagined possible. When I write, I truly lose track of where your words stop and mine begin. I am eternally grateful to you.

This book probably would not have been written had not Pastor Charles Green decided, some 25 years ago, to become a father to the fatherless and take me under his wing. To this day, when I hurt, he is always there to guide me with great wisdom and compassion. I hope I have grown up to make you proud.

I would also like to thank so many people who gave a chance to an unknown author and helped make my first book, *Money Came by the House the Other Day*, a success. Vijoya Chappelear and The Harvest Show, Pat Robertson and The 700 Club, Benny Hinn and This Is Your Day, and James Robison and Life Today are a few. I deeply appreciate your help.

I also want to thank Oral Roberts. Perhaps no man has done more to define the charismatic movement in the last 50 years than Pastor Roberts. Yet, when a stranger came knocking on his door for guidance, he went out of his way to help, to mentor, and to encourage. May the Lord continue to bless you and Mrs. Roberts.

Finally, on my knees, I thank the Holy Spirit. Whenever I'm finally quiet enough, You are always there to direct, to reveal, to guide, and to love. My prayer is that this book brings glory to You.

ENDORSEMENTS

"Filled with practical insights and Biblical truths, this inspirational book by Robert Katz will help to equip you with the tools and understanding you need to experience financial freedom. His balanced, Bible-based approach will bring financial freedom and blessing to your life as you obey God's principles."

—Benny Hinn
Founder/Pastor
World Healing Center Church/Benny Hinn Ministries

"When you think about your financial situation are you anxious, fearful or simply depressed? Using concrete biblical principles, Robert Katz steers you toward the path to financial freedom and gives you tangible tools to obtain 'true' wealth that's eternal."

—Kristi Watts
Co-host *The 700 Club*

I believe that this is one of the most balanced, scripturally sound, and powerful books available about prosperity the way God intended. In this book, Bob explains the foundations and daily courses of action to achieve Biblical prosperity in terms of why and how.

Bob is a purveyor of solid Biblical truth who has a deep understanding of Kingdom secrets of real prosperity the way God intended for us to live in the here and now, and the hereafter. I can only pray that as you turn the pages of this book you will allow yourself to be challenged to receive and apply the wisdom you will find.

—Vijoya Chappelear
Co-host, *The Harvest Show*, LeSEA Broadcasting

Robert Katz has written a delightful, informative and disturbing book. He does not cover us up with endless theological statements. What he does do is this—he shines the Light of God's Word on our lives. Without condemning us, he pulls the cover off of greed, unbelief, selfishness and fear.

"Biblical Roads to Financial Freedom" is not about doctrine. It is about living and enjoying life today—coming under the abundant blessing of God in this life and laying up treasures in the life to come.

You are about to learn the real meaning of life—and how to live it.

—Dr. Charles Green
Founding Pastor – Faith Church
New Orleans, La.

I am grateful that our God has allowed Bob to minister to and through our fellowship of believers. He is impacting the Body of Christ with clear words of wisdom in scriptural stewardship. He will stir your heart both to repent of past foolishness in handling finances and reaching for the eternal. This book will remind you that all that you possess was given for the purpose of glorifying your God. Balance is given in daily decisions and eternal consequences. I believe your life will increase materially and in Godly influence.

—Pastor Michael Millé
White Dove Fellowship Church

CONTENTS

About the Authors 13

Foreword 15

Introduction 17

PART ONE: THE KINGDOM OF GOD 21

Chapter 1.   House of Mirrors
"Poor Reflections, Partial Tales" 23

Chapter 2.   The Third Seed
"Enter Deceit" 33

Chapter 3.   The Runner
"It Just Couldn't Be That Simple" 47

Chapter 4.   Biblical Prosperity
"How Do I Get There From Here?" 55

Chapter 5.   It All Begins With Tithes and Offerings
"The Keys to Supernatural Release" 65

Chapter 6.   Beware of Debt
"Devilish Distraction" 71

Chapter 7.   Seek Godly Wisdom
"He Still Answers All" 77

Chapter 8.   Be Diligent About the Basics
"Knowing the Condition of Your Flocks" 81

Chapter 9.   Diversify
"Apples and Baskets" 89

Chapter 10. Avoid the Schemes and Dreams of Man
"But It Sounded So Good" 93

Chapter 11. Provide for the Future
"So Noah, Why the Big Boat?" 97

Chapter 12. Find Someone to Whom You Will Be Accountable
"We All Need Covering" .101

Chapter 13. Live a Life of Character, Discipline, and Honesty
"What Would Jesus Do?" 105

Chapter 14. Embrace Great Exploits
"Impossible, Difficult, Done" 109

Chapter 15. Wonderful Counselor
"The Holy Spirit" 115

Chapter 16. A Prophet and a King
"Abraham and Solomon" 131

PART TWO: THE KINGDOM OF HEAVEN 147

Chapter 17. Pauper in Paradise
"What I Dread the Most" 149

Chapter 18. Real Meat By-Products
"The Meaning of Life" 157

Chapter 19. Grave Consequences
"Choose Ye This day" 165

Epilogue Do You Know Jesus? 169

Appendix 171

Endnotes 183

ABOUT THE AUTHORS

Robert W. Katz has been a partner in New Orleans-based certified public accounting firms for the last 25 years. His areas of specialty include personal financial planning, tax and estate planning, and health care consulting. He received his bachelor's degree from Louisiana State University and his master's degree from the University of New Orleans. He is a certified public accountant and a registered investment advisor. Bob is the author of *The Physician's Survival Guide to the Business of Medicine*; *The Family Practitioner's Survival Guide to the Business of Medicine*; and the well-received book on Christian financial planning, *Money Came by the House the Other Day*.

This book was born of his deep desire to serve the Lord by offering Bible-based wisdom on godly stewardship and biblical prosperity.

Bob is a frequent teacher at churches and conferences and is often a guest on Christian television shows such as *This Is Your Day* with Benny Hinn, *The 700 Club* with Pat Robertson, *Life Today* with James Robison, and *The Harvest Show*.

He resides in New Orleans with his wife, Jamie, and their two children.

Jamie Katz is a graduate of Loyola University in New Orleans with a degree in communications. Bob and Jamie have been married for 20 years. Jamie enjoys being a homemaker and homeschooling their two children, Stephanie and Jonathan.

Jamie would like to acknowledge and thank God for how greatly she has been blessed with a heritage in the Lord and with the teaching of the Word that she has received from her pastor, Michael Millé, sister Elaine Millé, and Joyce Meyer. In addition to writing with her husband, Jamie also enjoys intercessory prayer and teaching the Word of God.

FOREWORD

It is often amazing how the Lord brings circumstances full circle.

I first met Bob Katz two years ago when he was a guest on the 700 Club discussing his first book *Money Came by the House the Other Day*. But, that meeting had been set in motion twenty-five years earlier. At that time Bob was an ex-Marine, graduate student, who was Jewish, lost and searching. One evening as he was flipping through the channels he came across the 700 Club. He told me that at first he would watch the show to mock it, but that little by little the love of the Lord drew him in. One night as he was watching the show, he just "knew" that the person I was describing was him. Alone, in his apartment, he dropped to his knees and gave his life to Christ…and that life has been forever changed.

Now, fast forward twenty-five years.

Bob has been a frequent guest on the 700 Club, his first book which dealt with Christian financial planning and stewardship has been well received and he has asked me to write the foreword to his new book. We have come full circle.

Biblical Roads to Financial Freedom continues on from where Bob's first book ended. It is a poignant reminder that one of satan's most vicious tools to rob us of prosperity on earth and treasure in heaven is the deceitfulness of wealth.

Part I of the book, The Kingdom of God, discusses the top ten Biblical financial principles that Christians most often violate. These chapters offer spiritual insight and practical scripture advice based on how to deal with the most common pitfalls of financial stewardship.

Part II of this book, The Kingdom of Heaven, was perhaps the most compelling part for me. In the last three chapters of this book, Bob speaks to the seldom discussed, but vitally important topic of storing eternal treasure in heaven.

In the midst of this high tech, fast paced world, the ending of this book grabs us and makes us ask the questions every Christian should be asking, "What treasure am I storing on the other side that will stand the test of His fire? What am I sowing now that will reap an eternal reward?" The answers to these questions are critically important to every believer's life, both now and for eternity.

For those of you who are looking for a good book which offers simple steps to attaining prosperity on earth and storing treasure in heaven it is a pleasure for me to highly recommend *Biblical Roads to Financial Freedom* to you.

—Pat Robertson
The 700 Club

INTRODUCTION

In November 2001 I had just finished a week of interviews with Pastor Benny Hinn on his television show, *This Is Your Day*. We had been discussing my first Christian book on stewardship, *Money Came by the House the Other Day*. Pastor Hinn had been a delight to work with, and I was very pleased with the way the shows had gone. I had no idea that the Lord was about to take me through a season that would seem to me to be the worst year of my entire life.

During this season of trial and revelation, the Lord dealt with me about many areas in my life that needed to change if I were to serve Him at a higher level. He also began to reveal to me the need for this book. The Lord explained that the purpose of my first book had been to instruct people on how to be better stewards of those things that He had temporarily entrusted to their care. He went on to show me, however, that His people are still being terribly deceived by wealth.

We forget that we are only *temporary caretakers*—that it all *belongs* to Him. We have become so focused with acquiring "things" that we have forgotten how soon they all disappear. We have become so fixed on obtaining earthly treasure that we have ignored His command to store true treasure in Heaven. We pour all of our waking hours into a quest for the seen, totally ignoring the unseen. We covet the temporal and turn our backs on the eternal, breaking His heart along the way.

His people are entering Heaven without having stored eternal treasure. They are literally **paupers in Paradise**, for eternity. The Lord began to instruct me to write a book to warn His people.

The purpose of this book is twofold. The first part of the book is instruction on becoming better stewards here on earth—not to learn how to acquire greater wealth, but to be freed from the deceitfulness of wealth so that we can fulfill the Lord's true purpose for our lives. Scripture tells us that the Lord has prepared in advance *good works* for each of us to accomplish during our time on earth. We are given one life, one brief chance, to accomplish these works. *The stakes are eternal.* Yet the lives of many of us are so weighed down by the cares of this world that we squander that chance and lose much of our eternal reward.

The second part of the book teaches us what Scripture has to say about storing treasure in Heaven. We are created to rule and reign with the Lord for all eternity, and at this very moment we are in training to do so. The Lord is using the material realm to teach us about the spiritual, the seen things to teach us about the unseen, and the momentary to teach us about the eternal. Every decision we make we will see again in the light of His perfect judgment. The eternal consequences of each act of stewardship will be revealed to us by the Lord, and we will be rewarded accordingly. It is an awesome truth to consider.

For many months the Lord revealed to me the need for this book and what He wanted in it, but I did not feel a release to sit down and complete it. Then in the latter part of 2002 I was reading *The Vision* by Rick Joyner. Relating a vision given to him by the Lord, Pastor Joyner describes an aristocracy in Heaven based on works. Those who have wasted their earthly lives find themselves on the outer edges of Heaven for eternity.

Pastor Joyner wrote,

"The rewards for our earthly lives are the eternal positions that we will have forever. This great multitude are those whom the Lord called 'foolish virgins.' We knew the Lord and trusted in His cross for salvation, but we lived for ourselves more than we really lived for Him. We did not keep our vessels filled with the oil of the Holy Spirit. We have eternal life, but we wasted our lives on earth."[1]

As I read this paragraph, I finally felt the Lord's release.

My prayer is that as you read, this book will touch your spirit and create a burning desire in your heart to want to accomplish His eternal purpose for your life. I hope that it lifts your vision from your temporary situation on earth to your eternal situation in Heaven. May you walk in assurance that:

Though outwardly we are wasting away, yet inwardly we are being renewed day by day. For our light and momentary troubles are achieving for us an eternal glory that far outweighs them all. So we fix our eyes not on what is seen, but on what is unseen. For what is seen is temporary, but what is unseen is eternal.

2 Corinthians 4:16b-18

Part One

THE KINGDOM OF GOD

Now we see but a poor reflection as in a mirror; then we shall see face to face. Now I know in part; then I shall know fully, even as I am fully known.

1 Corinthians 13:12

— 1 —

HOUSE OF MIRRORS

"Poor Reflections, Partial Tales"

"Because I love her."

That's the answer you whisper to the unasked question, *Why am I doing this?*

It's Saturday afternoon. The lawn has been mowed, and its borders have been edged with great precision. Weeds have been unmercifully plucked, bundled, and banished from the flower beds. The clothes have been picked up from the cleaners, and the refrigerator has been stocked with food. The couch is calling to you. You long to turn on the television and let the drone of a mindless show become background music for a nice long nap. After all, that is why the Lord invented Saturday afternoons!

But then your beautiful bride of 19 years comes in and sits next to you with that smile on her face. You think, *I should have lain down earlier; I should have had my eyes closed.*

She says, "Honey, we really need an end table to go with this couch…and it's such a beautiful afternoon…wouldn't it be fun for the two of us to go antiquing?"

Antiquing? You didn't even know it was a verb.

She gently puts her arms around your neck and kisses you. "Come on—if we stay here you'll just fall asleep on the couch."

"Yes, exactly. That's not a bad thing…that actually was my plan, to fall asleep peacefully on the couch."

A second hug, a second kiss. "Come on, please, it wouldn't be any fun to go by myself." After all these years you don't know how she does it, but her eyes actually smile. And you are up and off, antiquing.

"Why does it smell so bad in here?"

"It doesn't smell bad, it smells musty—that's the smell of age."

"I hope I don't smell like that as I age."

"Shush, help me look for an end table."

Actually, you know that she's not looking for an end table; she's looking to shop. After many years of marital ignorance you have finally discovered the difference. Shopping is the experience. It is the wandering up and down aisles, looking at everything. It's the touching, the talking, the "Isn't this pretty?" and the "Wouldn't that be nice?" To her, if shopping is done properly, the table is merely the period at the end of a beautiful sentence.

To you the end table is the sentence.

And antique shopping should be a short sentence.

Your recollection of antique stores is that the aisles are narrow and that you are always one step away from breaking something that costs more than you make in a year. Antique stores make no economic sense. The more decrepit the item, the more useless, the worse its condition…the more it costs. Besides, the whole process is so confusing. How many Louis' and Henry's can there be? Who are Chip and Dale anyway? Why would lions have balls in their feet? Empire, Victorian, Neoclassical, English, French provincial, early American…most of it just looks like….

"May I help you?"

A kindly old gentleman, who looks like something of an antique himself, has shuffled up to you. He's wearing those thick rubber-soled shoes that people who are on their feet a lot wear. His suit is rumpled, but under it is a crisp white shirt and a real bow tie. In the center of his chest a pair of reading glasses hang suspended on an old pewter chain.

"Is there something in particular you are looking for?"

You want to say, *No, go away*, but what you hear is her voice. "Everything here is so lovely. But we're looking for an end table."

"And where will it be placed?"

You want to say, *Next to the couch I should be sleeping on*, but again she answers, "In our living room next to the couch. Nothing too formal. I love the French country look...like this one, but maybe not as large. Do you have any others like this?"

"Of course. Somewhere in this store we have exactly what everyone is looking for. We always do."

Then he turns to you. Rubbing his chin gently he just stares. His eyes are kind. A compassionate smile rests on the corners of his mouth, as if he knows the slow torture you are silently enduring.

"How about you, sir, anything in particular that you are seeking today?"

You want to say...but he continues.

"You know, I believe we do have something that you would find very interesting. In fact, I'd be delighted to show your wife around the store, while you peruse our back room. Allow me..."

Putting his hand on your shoulder, he points you to the back of the store. "Go all the way to the end of this aisle, then turn right. Then go all the way to the end of the corridor and you'll see a room. Go on in—I think you'll be fascinated by what you find. We'll come and get you in a little while."

"Go ahead, honey. It sounds intriguing. Take your time; that way I won't feel rushed."

You walk to the rear of the store, hoping that the back room is filled with televisions and recliners. Turning right, you see the entrance. Above the doorway is a sign that reads:

The Mirror Room
Poor Reflections, Partial Tales

The mirror room? Why on earth would that old guy send you to roam around in a room full of mirrors? As you enter the room and your eyes begin to adjust to the dim light, you are baffled by what you see. Dozens of mirrors have been randomly placed on the walls, on pedestals, some even suspended from the ceiling. There are square ones with beveled edges and rectangles with gilded frames—some simple, some ornate, in various sizes—each capturing the same light, but offering back its own unique reflection.

Stepping in front of one of the mirrors, you notice that something appears to be etched in the glass. As you center yourself on the mirror, the reflection of a mighty king stares back at you. Behind him, as far as the eye can see, are the treasures of his kingdom. His palaces are filled with gold and silver. Vineyards and gardens and orchards swell with ripe delicacies. His stables house the best horses in the world; his pens hold the finest sheep and cattle. At his feet a river of men bow, paying homage to his wisdom and power.

You think to yourself that it's an odd mirror. You've seen painted mirrors before, but none using this technique. As you move a little to one side, trying to figure out how the artist did what he did, a strange thing happens. The whole scene changes before your eyes, as if it's a living hologram. The once grand king begins to age. His clothes fade in color; his gardens and orchards become neglected and overgrown. The river of men paying homage that once ran at his feet turns into hundreds of small streams running in every direction.

Startled, you begin to back away from the mirror. As you move, the king appears to drop to his knees. The light is gone from his eyes. His thin, frail body is barely able to support the weight of his royal garments. His pale white hands are reaching out to you. From somewhere you sense a voice crying out, "Meaningless, meaning-less...meaningless."

Quickly you back away until your angle to the mirror is so acute that the reflection disappears.

"What's going on here?" you murmur to yourself.

That salesman must be having some fun, at your expense, with some very special, special effects. There is some trick, some projection system you cannot see, some logical explanation as to why one moment you see a mighty king and the next an old man in misery. While you are mulling this over, a rather small mirror on a black pedestal just a few feet away catches your eye.

Cautiously you walk over to it.

Once again a scene is revealed in the silvered glass. This time it reflects an ancient temple. Massive stone walls push out to the four corners of the mirror. The splendor of a grand marble colonnade draws your gaze to the temple's elegant entrance. Beside the door sits an ornately carved offering box of highly polished acacia. Skilled craftsmen constructed the box to appear seamless. Its hinges and lock are inlaid with gold. The box rests on a burnished bronze table.

Approaching the table is an old woman. Next to the beauty of the offering box she is almost invisible. Her clothes are patched, frayed, and filthy. You can't see her eyes because they are cast down to the ground. Her shoulders are stooped forward, permanently rounded by a lifetime of submission. You have to strain to see, but you notice two small copper coins in her tiny outstretched hand.

You are almost afraid to move.

Once again you shift your viewing angle, and once again the scene changes dramatically.

Before your eyes the temple crumbles and disappears. It is replaced by a golden street bordered by the most magnificent gardens you have ever seene. The flowers are translucent, their colors so vibrant that they seem to burst from the mirror. Walking down the street is a beautiful woman. Her face bears a radiant smile, her hair shines golden, and she is clothed in a beautiful robe. At first, you don't recognize her, but then you see—it is the old woman.

Again, you hear a voice that seems to call from within you—a still small voice whispering, "She gave more than all the others."

Although there is no one in the room you answer back, "She gave more of what than all of the others? Give me a break. These are trick mirrors. This is sleight of hand, science fiction hocus pocus. I don't know exactly how I'm being deceived here, but I'm going to find out what's going on."

Defiantly you place yourself in front of a large square mirror hanging from the ceiling by two golden wires. At first, the grotesqueness of its scene makes you turn your head away. Lying at the bottom of a mirror, in the middle of a dirt road, is a dying beggar. Except for a loincloth he is naked. His ribs push up his sallow skin like a row of bony gravestones. Flies cover his face, but he is too weak to brush them away...or to fend off the dogs licking at his sores.

Across the road is a beautiful home. Through the window you see an obviously wealthy man sitting at his table quietly eating.

Preoccupied with the business of the day, he is unaware of the beggar's plight.

As with all of the other mirrors you take a little step to slightly shift your perspective. In the blink of your eye, the beggar and the rich man have eternally changed places. You draw back in horror to see the wealthy man in hell screaming out in eternal torment. Then you see the beggar, restored and resting in the arms of an angel.

Again, that voice inside of you calls out, a little louder this time, "Tell them, tell them, tell them, before it is too late."

The mirror room is no longer fun. The novelty of trying to uncover the deception has worn off. You wonder to yourself, "Tell them *what*? What did the rich man do to deserve hell? He was just sitting there." You have had enough. It is time to get your wife and get out of the antique store. But as you turn to leave, you notice that the far wall has only one mirror on it. Why, in this room crammed full of mirrors, is that one all by itself?

The solitary mirror is simple, compared with the other mirrors, and reveals a common scene—the Crucifixion. On a hill stand three crosses. On one of them is nailed the badly beaten body of Jesus Christ. His head hangs lifeless; death has already taken Him.

Finally you've figured it out. Now it all makes sense. That old salesman is some kind of religious nut. All the mirrors, the shifting scenes, the whole room is one big set-up to lead you to some sort of religious revelation. No doubt that as you change your viewing angle, this scene, too, will change before your very eyes. No doubt the cross will give way to a beautiful scene of Heaven, which is intended to move you deeply.

Shifting your position you look again at Jesus. But nothing happens. His limp body continues to hang on the cross. Wait a minute. You move again—still nothing—and again from left to right, from top to bottom. The scene never changes. Maybe it's broken. Grabbing the mirror's frame, you shake it, thinking, "Change, change, show me Heaven, and let me go home!"

But the only sound you hear comes from deep within your chest, "I never knew you."

You run out of the room and find your wife paying for an end table.

"Oh, there you are. Look what I've found! Won't it be just perfect next to the couch?"

"Oh, yeah, just perfect. Are you ready to go?"

The salesman hands your wife her receipt and then shuffles up next to you. "And how about you, sir—did you enjoy the back room?"

"It was okay, but it wasn't really what I was looking for."

Still others, like seed sown among thorns, hear the word; but the worries of this life, the deceitfulness of wealth and the desires for other things come in and choke the word, making it unfruitful.

Mark 4:18-19

The Third Seed

"Enter Deceit"

Has prosperity ever deceived you? Has the pursuit of wealth, like the vanishing images in a mirror, left you feeling empty and disillusioned?

If the answer is yes, you are not alone. The wealthiest and wisest man who ever lived spent the last days of his life anguishing over the deceitfulness of riches. Great King Solomon's voice travels across the centuries, lamenting, "meaningless, meaningless…meaningless." In the Book of Ecclesiastes he cries out that all of his accomplishments and all of his wealth, at the end of the day, amount to no more than a chasing of the wind. Listen in:

I undertook great projects: I built houses for myself and planted vineyards. I made gardens and parks and planted all kinds of fruit trees in them. I made reservoirs to water groves of flourishing trees. I bought male and female slaves and had other slaves who were born in my house. I also owned more herds and flocks than anyone in Jerusalem before me. I amassed silver and gold for myself, and the treasure of kings and provinces. I acquired men and women singers, and a harem as well—the delights of the heart of man. I became greater by far than anyone in Jerusalem before me. In all this my wisdom stayed with me. I denied myself nothing my eyes desired; I refused my heart no pleasure. My heart took delight in all my work, and this was the reward for all my labor. **Yet when I surveyed all that my hands had done and what I had toiled to achieve, everything was meaningless, a chasing after the wind; nothing was gained under the sun.**

Ecclesiastes 2:4-11

Allow yourself to truly feel the anguish in the words Solomon used to describe the fruit of the works of his entire life: "...*meaningless, a chasing after the wind; nothing was gained....*" I believe that he was really trying to tell us, "Don't hold on to anything too tightly...it's all on loan."

It's sobering and confusing. How was the wisest man who ever lived so deceived by the pursuit of prosperity? If this most insightful of men was deceived by wealth, what chance do we have?

Next, consider the case of the poor widow found in the Book of Luke. About her two copper coins Jesus said, "This poor widow has put in more than all the others" (Lk. 21:3b). It is fair to ask, "More of what?" It wasn't money. Jerusalem's magnificent temple was built on the gold of wealthy patrons, not on the copper coins of elderly widows. So more of what? More time, more prayers, more of her heart...we really don't know. Scripture is silent, yet her story is eternal.

Consider Lazarus and the rich man. This is such a powerful story that I ask you to bear with me and read it in its entirety:

There was a rich man who was dressed in purple and fine linen and lived in luxury every day. At his gate was laid a beggar named Lazarus, covered with sores and longing to eat

34

what fell from the rich man's table. Even the dogs came and licked his sores.

The time came when the beggar died and the angels carried him to Abraham's side. The rich man also died and was buried. In hell, where he was in torment, he looked up and saw Abraham far away, with Lazarus by his side. So he called to him, "Father Abraham, have pity on me and send Lazarus to dip the tip of his finger in water and cool my tongue, because I am in agony in this fire."

But Abraham replied, "Son remember that in your lifetime you received your good things, while Lazarus received bad things, but now he is comforted here and you are in agony. And besides all this, between us and you a great chasm has been fixed, so that those who want to go from here to you cannot, nor can anyone cross over from there to us."

He answered, "Then I beg you, father, send Lazarus to my father's house, for I have five brothers. Let him warn them, so that they will not also come to this place of torment."

Abraham replied, "They have Moses and the Prophets; let them listen to them."

"No, father Abraham," he said, "but if someone from the dead goes to them, they will repent."

He said to him, "If they do not listen to Moses and the Prophets, they will not be convinced even if someone rises from the dead."

Luke 16:19-31

Now, let me ask you a question. Why is the rich man in hell?

Be careful before you answer, because once again Scripture is surprisingly silent. Nowhere in Scripture do we read that he was an evil

35

man or a terrible sinner who got what he deserved. He may have been a tithe paying, synagogue attending, law keeping, normal run-of-the-day businessman. If the issue was callousness, why doesn't Scripture tell us that the rich man ignored Lazarus's needs or looked down on him with contempt? Was his crime simply that he was rich? I can't find any scriptural reference to "the sin of wealth."

If being wealthy is a sin, we had all better drop to our knees in repentance. I suspect, comparatively speaking, that almost everyone in the United States is a rich person in a world of Lazaruses. And, but for the grace of Christ, we all stand teetering at the edge of the rich man's flaming pit. Indeed it is very humbling and scary to ponder why the rich man was in hell.

It is puzzling, this notion of wealth and prosperity. God gave Solomon great wealth, and Solomon called it meaningless. A poor old woman gave two copper coins, and the same God called her gift abundant. A beggar goes to Heaven, a rich man to hell; and we receive no satisfactory explanation.

Clearly, something else is going on here besides the mere management of wealth. There must be something that affects our relationship with what we "own" that goes beyond the rules and regulations of the natural world. That something is the realization that the pursuit of prosperity is as much a spiritual battle as it is natural one. In the Book of Ephesians we are warned about this battle:

> For our struggle is not against flesh and blood, but against the rulers, against the authorities, against the powers of this dark world and against the spiritual forces of evil in the heavenly realms.

> Ephesians 6:12

The enemy's purpose is clearly revealed to us in the Gospel of John:

The thief comes only to steal and kill and destroy.

John 10:10a

Perhaps it is fear, perhaps familiarity, but something in us wants to read the above parables as children's stories. We want to believe that the powerful truths revealed by Jesus serve merely to illustrate a general lesson, rather than a personal message. The truth is that very little has changed in five thousand years. Every moment of every day, the deception of wealth leads real men and real women straight into the jaws of hell.

During the past 25 years, I have counseled with hundreds of Christian and non-Christians on matters of finance and stewardship. To me, it appears that we are living in a time when the deception of wealth is stronger than ever. For instance, recently I counseled with two couples. One couple had an annual income of $30,000; the other $350,000. What was interesting was how similar their situations were. Both couples were hopelessly in debt. Neither couple really understood how they got there. Both had a long list of culprits to blame for their situation. Neither list included satan. Both saw their dilemma as a worldly one that needed a worldly solution, not Holy Spirit intervention. Neither felt the choke hold of satan clamping down around their throats, ready to strangle them to their knees. To both, the problem appeared to be a simple one—they didn't have enough money.

Sadly, cases such as these are common, not isolated. I counsel with the poor and the privileged, the middle class and the millionaires. I have counseled with the ultra wealthy who tell me that they literally cannot sleep at night, because they are tormented by the fear of losing everything they have acquired. I have heard stories from so many "middle class" families who are reaping the financial chaos born of years of poor stewardship. Rich or poor, the symptoms of shoddy stewardship are the same: excessive debt, crumbling relationships, growing addictions, living in the future, a sense of hopelessness and of not being in control, *and a joyless, fruitless life*. Today, we have an army of God's children, most deceived, many bitter, drifting into their golden years with the only gold coming their way taking the form of a social security check. Angry with God, they feel that they have been double-crossed.

And they have been double-crossed, but not by God.

Please understand this vital point: *satan viciously uses the deceitfulness of wealth to bring double destruction upon the unwary.*

The First Destruction Comes in the Kingdom of God

The New Testament goes into great detail about two kingdoms, the Kingdom of God and the Kingdom of Heaven. It is important that we understand what the Lord means by each kingdom. The Kingdom of God is the supernatural life we were created to enjoy here and now, *on earth*, by living in and through the Holy Spirit.

> *For the Kingdom of God is not a matter of eating and drinking, but of righteousness, peace and joy in the Holy Spirit, because anyone who serves Christ in this way is pleasing to God and approved by men.*
>
> Romans 14:17-18

When Christ returned to Heaven, He sent the Holy Spirit to help us boldly abide in the Kingdom of God during our time on earth. The believer's life on earth is meant to glorify God, and should be recognized by its abundant joy, peace, and righteousness. Christ, through the work of the Holy Spirit, has arranged a *safe harbor* for us here on earth. That safe harbor is the Kingdom of God. It is in the Holy Spirit that we will find a peace beyond understanding, regardless of our circumstances. But it is hard for us to remain in the Kingdom of God and walk in the Spirit, because satan uses temptations and deceptions to constantly war against our flesh, our souls, and our minds.

> *The acts of the sinful nature are obvious: sexual immorality, impurity and debauchery; idolatry and witchcraft; hatred, discord, jealousy, fits of rage, selfish ambition, dissensions, factions and envy; drunkenness, orgies, and the like. I warn you, as I did before, that those who live like this will not inherit the* **kingdom of God**

Galatians 5:19-21

Obviously, Paul was not speaking of Heaven in the verse above; if he were, **no one** would go to Heaven. He was referring to our life on earth, the Kingdom of God. The Lord is saying that we can easily lose the fullness of the life that He intended for us on earth if we continually allow our flesh (minds, thoughts, emotions) to pull us out of relationship with the Holy Spirit. Knowing this, satan will use whatever means are necessary to destroy our relationship with the Holy Spirit and keep us from abiding in the super natural realm of the Kingdom of God. Sadly, in this country, one of satan's most powerful tools is to distract us from God's perfect will for our lives by luring us with the false promises of wealth.

The first destruction, the deceitfulness of wealth, takes place here on earth, in the Kingdom of God. Both the believer and the unsaved can fall victim to it. It is the third seed described by Jesus in His parable of the sower:

> *The one who received the seed that fell among the thorns is the man who hears the word, but the worries of this life and the deceitfulness of wealth choke it, making it unfruitful.*

Matthew 13:22

Satan initially uses the deceitfulness of wealth to try to draw people away from receiving their salvation. If he succeeds, these people pay an eternal price. Separated from Christ for eternity, they will abide in a place of hopelessness, despair, and torture that we cannot fathom.

But the believer is not immune from satan's intended destruction. If satan can't take your eternal spirit to hell, he will do all that he can to make your years on earth seem like hell. His attacks will be meant to keep you out of the Kingdom of God and out of relationship with the Holy Spirit. Once he has accomplished these goals, there will be no peace beyond understanding, no joy, no light yoke—and worst of all, you will produce no lasting fruit.

The Second Destruction Comes in the Kingdom of Heaven

The second destruction brought about by the deception of wealth is seldom discussed, but even more tragic. This deception involves the eternal Kingdom of Heaven.

In my 25 years of financial counseling, no one has ever once asked me for advice on storing up his or her treasures in Heaven.

Think about it. Our life on earth is approximately 80 years. No one would argue with Job when he says, "Naked I came from my mother's womb, and naked I will depart" (Job 1:20). Yet it seems that our entire focus is upon acquiring what does not last. We have believed the world's message and defiantly ignored Christ's clear instruction:

Do not store up for yourselves treasures on earth, where moth and rust destroy, and where thieves break in and steal. But store up for yourselves treasures in heaven, where moth and rust do not destroy, and where thieves do not break in and steal.

Matthew 6:19-20

The second deception of wealth is the most devastating because the loss is eternal. I can't begin to fathom that day—when we stand before the Lord, and He reveals the eternal rewards that we have lost because we chose to chase after the temporal. Scripture is so clear on this point: God has an *eternal* purpose for your life that is outside the calendar of your years on earth.

> *For we are...created in Christ Jesus to do good works, which*
> *God prepared in advance for us to do.*
>
> Ephesians 2:10

> *The world and its desires pass away, but the man who does*
> *the will of God lives forever.*
>
> 1 John 2:17

Revelation 7:17b tells us, "God will wipe away every tear from their eyes." I know that among those tears will be our bitter tears of regret over the eternal treasure we have lost by failing to accomplish what we had been called to do on earth. They will be the devastating tears of what might have been, had we abided in the Kingdom of God on earth. Only the compassion and mercy of Christ will be able wipe away these tears.

It is not as if we have not been warned. The very first gospel points us to that day:

> *For the Son of Man is going to come in His Father's glory with*
> *His angels, and then He will reward each person according to*
> *what he has done.*
>
> Matthew 16:27

In Corinthians, Paul implores us not to become paupers in paradise:

> *If any man builds on this foundation using gold, silver, costly*
> *stones, wood, hay or straw, his work will be shown for what*

*it is, because the Day will bring it to light. It will be revealed
with fire, and the fire will test the quality of each man's work.
If what he has built survives, he will receive his reward. If it
is burned up, he will suffer loss; he himself will be saved, but
only as one escaping through the flames.*

1 Corinthians 3:12-15

And Revelation confirms this truth one final time:

*I am He who searches hearts and minds, and I will repay each
of you according to your deeds.*

Revelation 2:23b.

Let me make myself very clear regarding this second destruction.
I am not talking about someone's eternal salvation being in jeopardy.
Salvation is accepting the blood of Christ plus nothing. I am speaking
about the treasures in Heaven we are failing to store up while here on
earth. In Heaven, the Lord won't be asking us about our business
deals or our stocks and bonds. He won't care about the house we lived
in, the car we drove, or how close to the front we sat in church. I suspect His questions will be more along these lines, "How did you love
the people that I put into your life each day? Did your love produce
lasting fruit? Did you do My will for your life?"

*For you were once darkness, but now you are light in the
Lord. Live as children of light (for the fruit of the light consists in all goodness, righteousness and truth) and find out
what pleases the Lord. Have nothing to do with the fruitless
deeds of darkness, but rather expose them.*

Ephesians 5:8-11

You see, biblical prosperity is really a journey. It begins in the
Kingdom of God and ends in the Kingdom of Heaven. To spend all of
our time seeking the here-and-now "promises" of the Bible is to see

only a poor temporal reflection in a mirror. To know fully we must lift our eyes and our hearts to the eternal Kingdom of Heaven.

This book is meant to help guide you on this journey. Its purpose is twofold: first, to discuss stewardship in the Kingdom of God; and, second, to guide us toward our goal of staying vigilant in our pursuit of glorifying God and storing lasting treasure in the Kingdom of Heaven.

Scripture reveals the ultimate goal of the journey; to stand face to face with the Lord and hear Him declare,

Well done, good and faithful servant! You have been faithful with a few things; I will put you in charge of many things. Come and share your master's happiness!

Matthew 25:2

BIBLICAL BASICS

1. To avoid being deceived by wealth, we must understand that the battle for godly stewardship is fought in both the natural and the spiritual realm.

2. We have an enemy, satan, whose purposes are to prevent salvation, destroy lives, and keep us from doing God's will. Creating financial havoc is one of his primary methods.

3. Satan uses the deceitfulness of wealth against the unsaved to steal their eternal salvation.

4. If you are saved, satan will try to use the deceitfulness of wealth to make your life on earth miserable, and to keep you from storing eternal treasure in the Kingdom of Heaven.

5. Our purpose on earth is to complete those good works that the Lord prepared in advance for us to do, thereby storing up abundant eternal treasure in Heaven.

Then a great and powerful wind tore the mountains apart and shattered the rocks before the Lord, but the Lord was not in the wind. After the wind there was an earthquake, but the Lord was not in the earthquake. After the earthquake came a fire, but the Lord was not in the fire. And after the fire came a gentle whisper.

1 Kings 19:11b-12

— 3 —

THE RUNNER

"It Just Couldn't Be That Simple"

The October wind beat against his face as he veered off the main road and ran onto the valley trail. He could see that the trail was an unrelenting incline that stretched for several miles and then converged into an even steeper mountain path. His thigh muscles were already burning and his lungs labored to breathe in fresh air, but he pushed on. He had been told that this was the path.

Just ahead he saw a clearing beside the trail and thought that perhaps this is it. Perhaps his search was about to end. As he approached the site, he noticed a man sitting in the middle of a circle that had been scratched into the red clay dirt. The runner slowed to a walk and approached the stranger.

"Are you the one?"

The stranger was sitting in the middle of the circle, peacefully chanting to himself and gently swaying back and forth like the branches of a willow tree on a fall morning. He was surrounded by candles and his eyes were closed. When he heard the voice of the runner he held up his left hand and without opening his eyes called out, "Do not enter the circle."

The runner stopped at the edge of the circle and appealed to him once again. "But I've come all this way and I must know—are you the one?"

The stranger jumped to his feet and dashed around the circle, crying, "Bad karma, bad karma, bad karma." Soon he became winded. He turned back to the runner, gasping for air, and said, "Do you see this?" He waved his thin arms around, pointing to the circumference of the circle that encased him. "This is the circle of mother earth. Before you can enter, before I should even speak to you, you must be in union with the cosmos. Go over there and hug that tree as a symbol of your desire to be one with creation!"

The runner stepped back and examined the small man in the purple robes before him. His body was frail, his face drawn and partially hidden by a scraggly salt-and-pepper beard. His head was barely covered by scant strands of hair arranged in no particular order; his feet were calloused and bare. He didn't give the impression of possessing the secrets of the universe. But the runner had come so far—what could possibly be the harm of indulging his peculiar request? He walked over to the edge of the clearing and quickly hugged the nearest tree.

The little man seemed pleased. He opened his arms and invited the runner to join him. "Please step into the universal circle of oneness."

The runner entered the circle, asking again, "Are you the one?"

"Which one would that be, my brother?"

"Are you the one who can tell me the meaning of life? I've come all this way...they told me that this was the path and when I saw you sitting..."

The stranger's bony little hand shot up into the air, interrupting him in mid-sentence. "Look around you. See your brother the deer, your sister the fish; breathe the air and visualize your oneness with the world around you. Here, watch me." And with that he began to roll in the dirt. "Come, join me as we reenter the womb of mother earth."

48

"But what about the meaning of life?"

The little man continued to lie on the ground like a fallen tree. His robe was covered with clay, and his thin hair was matted with leaves and twigs. He looked disappointed that the runner had not decided to join him in mother earth's womb. Spitting out a mouthful of dirt he responded, "The meaning of life?...hum, meaning of life. Well, that's really not my area...but I think you're on the right path. Up the trail a little farther, I think there may be someone who can help you. Here—take this with you on your journey, my brother."

He reached into his robe, pulled out a quartz crystal hanging from a leather necklace, and placed it around the runner's neck. He then squatted into the lotus position, closed his eyes and began softly chanting to himself once again.

Pushing onward, the runner came to the end of the valley trail and began to ascend the mountain path. His feet were blistering, and his legs were cut and bleeding from the thorn bushes growing along the path. But he knew that the importance of the quest was far greater than any pain or suffering he might have to endure.

By late afternoon he reached a plateau and noticed a cave in the face of the mountain. Cautiously, he approached the opening. He wondered if his exhaustion was playing tricks on him, because he could swear that the fragrance of sweet incense floated in the air around him.

"Well, don't just stand there—come on in," called a voice from inside the cave.

The voice was pleasant, and the runner was thirsty—so he obeyed.

The inside of the cave resembled a planetarium. Magnificent reproductions of constellations and astrological signs had been paint-ed on the stone Heaven above. Theatrical lighting made wisps of

smoke from burning incense appear to be clouds. Wonderfully sooth-
ing music that sounded like flowing water eased from speakers in the
corners of the cave.

He was greeted by a beautiful woman wearing a flowing white
gown. She sat casually behind a large granite table, shuffling a deck of
tarot cards.

"I knew you'd be here sooner or later. Come sit down." She pointed at the cards and motioned for him to join her at the table.

"Are you the one?"

"Which one would that be?"

"The one, the guru, the holder of all truth, the one who can tell me
the meaning of life?"

She rolled her eyes and laughed. "Guru? Such an archaic term, I
don't hear that one much anymore. Is that what that little weirdo in
the valley told you I was, a guru? Honey, this is a new age we're living
in now."

She reached across the table and patted the top of his hands in
sympathy. "Today we prefer terms such as channel guide, or psychic,
or astral projector."

"Yes, yes that's fine—but can you tell me the meaning of life?"

"Honey, if I can't I am sure that I can put you in touch with someone who can." She leaned across the table, putting her face within
inches of his. "Did you bring any money with you?"

He stood up to leave.

"What's your hurry? Got any dead relatives you'd like to talk to?"

As he backed up he tripped over an old crystal ball lying on the
cave floor.

"Why are you leaving so soon after having traveled such a long way? Would you like for me to separate your spirit from your body so you can travel through space and time?"

He turned around and started to run.

"Wait, come back—I'm doing a special on reincarnations this week. Pay to have one previous life revealed and the next one is free."

With the little remaining energy left in his weary body, the runner stumbled back down the mountain path. Night was beginning to close in on the valley as he made his way through it. Finally, he sprinted the last few hundred yards to the main road and collapsed onto its shoulder.

Physically drained and emotionally dejected, he walked back to town.

The path home took him past a little wooden church. It had been on that same corner for as long as he could remember, although he had never been inside it. The church's pastor, who was leaving for the evening, saw the runner and called to him, "You don't look well, my friend. Is there anything I can do for you?"

"I've just come from the valley. I've been searching for the meaning of life, and this is all I have to show for it." He pointed to his bruised and bleeding body and then held up the quartz pendant that the old man had given him.

The minister smiled at him. "The meaning of life? You mean to tell me that you suffered like that in order to find something so simple? Wait here a minute."

The minister walked over to his parked car, opened the door, pulled out a Bible and handed it to the young man. "This is the meaning of life. If you ever want to talk about it, I am always here."

He smiled at the young man again, got into his car, and drove away.

The runner walked to the corner, opened the book under the street light and read quietly to himself,

Ask and it will be given to you; seek and you will find; knock and the door will be opened to you. For everyone who asks receives; he who seeks finds; and to him who knocks, the door will be opened.

Matthew 7:7-8

He silently read the message one more time and walked home. When he got there he tossed the Bible on the table. *It just couldn't be that simple. Maybe in Tibet, up in the Himalayas there is someone who....*

Let your eyes look straight ahead, fix your gaze directly before you. Make level paths for your feet and take only ways that are firm. Do not swerve to the right or the left; keep your foot from evil.

Proverbs 4:25-27

— 4 —

BIBLICAL PROSPERITY

"How Do I Get There From Here?"

When it comes to your personal finances, have you ever felt like a lonely marathon runner? Has the race left you weary and exhausted? Do you feel that just when you see the finish line, it turns out to be a mirage? After you have run and run, mile after mile, do you look around only to find that you have been going in circles? So have we all.

I believe it is because most of us have lost sight of the Lord's plan for our lives in the Kingdom of God.

So, let's settle this issue once and for all.

Our eternal purpose on earth is not to amass fleeting wealth, it is to obtain *biblical prosperity*. Biblical prosperity is the ongoing process of *godly stewardship* and is comprised of three foundational concepts:

1. *Godly success*—first and foremost, achieving God's purpose for your life. The Lord has a distinct and wonderful plan for every believer's life. You are perfectly created for your unique purpose. When you commit your life to living in the midst of that plan and seek the Lord's direction as David described, "As the deer pants for steams of water, so my soul pants for you, O God. My soul thirsts for God, for the living God" (Ps. 42:1-2a), something miraculous begins to happen.

A supernatural release is placed upon your life. Doors that once were closed spring open, and deeds that were impossible suddenly are done. The Lord revealed the requirement for godly success to Joshua over five thousand years ago, and it remains unchanged for us today:

Do not let this Book of the Law depart from your mouth; meditate on it day and night, so that you may be careful to do everything written in it. Then you will be prosperous and successful.

Joshua 1:8

2. *Godly affluence and influence*—having all of the means necessary to accomplish the Lord's unique purpose for your life. The Lord will never call you and not equip you.

And my God will meet all your needs according to His glorious riches in Christ Jesus.

Philippians 4:19

If you are truly pursuing His plan for your life, the Lord will always bring into your life the funds and the people necessary to help you accomplish the task at hand. But there is a requirement that He will place upon you before releasing affluence and influence into your life.

*Seek first His kingdom and His righteousness, **and all these things will be given to you as well.***

Matthew 6:33

3. *Godly Freedom*—a supernatural release that you receive when you have purposed in your heart to serve God instead of money. It is at this point, when you have chosen to no longer worry about tomorrow, that the supernatural and the miraculous become commonplace in your life. This

freedom is not just the absence of fear and anxiety. It is a bold faith born of total dependence on the Lord.

Now the Lord is the Spirit, and where the Spirit of the Lord is, there is freedom.

2 Corinthians 3:17

So if the Son sets you free, you will be free indeed.

John 8:36

The Fruit Factor

A simple test to see if you are on the road to biblical prosperity is to look at the *fruit of the Spirit* in your life. The Lord has allowed many people in this world to have success and wealth. The driving purpose of their lives is to obtain *more*. As they turn their backs on the Lord in the pursuit of *more*, He releases them to the desires of their sinful hearts. They may have obtained prosperity, but not biblical prosperity. While they look good on the outside, if you could see the inner man you would find souls tormented by fear, anxiety, greed, anger, distrust, and every sort of evil spirit. With biblical prosperity comes the Lord's gifts of the fruit of the Spirit:

But the fruit of the Spirit is love, joy, peace, patience, kindness, goodness, faithfulness, gentleness and self-control.

Galatians 5:22-23a

because,

The blessing of the Lord brings wealth, and He adds no trouble to it.

Proverbs 10:22

Is the fruit of the Spirit evident in your life? If the answer is yes, you are on the road to biblical prosperity. You can expect the Lord to

57

continually urge you farther down the road by intensifying your lessons in stewardship.

Godly Stewardship

We travel the road to biblical prosperity by our unceasing efforts to mature as godly stewards.

I cannot overemphasize how important it is to understand the concept of godly stewardship. A steward is someone who has been placed in charge of something that does not belong to him. A steward is a temporary caretaker. We are only temporary stewards of the Lord's property while here on this earth. Nothing of this earth will ever belong to us, but we will eternally answer for how we took care of everything the Lord entrusted to us. If you have any doubt about how seriously the Lord views the principle of biblical stewardship, read the parable of the talents found in Matthew 25:14-30:

> *Again, it will be like a man going on a journey, who called his servants and entrusted his property to them. To one he gave five talents of money, to another two talents, and to another one talent, each according to his ability. Then he went on his journey. The man who had received the five talents went at once and put his money to work and gained five more. So also, the one with the two talents gained two more. But the man who had received the one talent went off, dug a hole in the ground and hid his master's money.*
>
> *After a long time the master of those servants returned and settled accounts with them. The man who had received the*

five talents brought the other five. "Master," he said, "you entrusted me with five talents. See, I have gained five more."

His master replied, "Well done, good and faithful servant! You have been faithful with a few things; I will put you in charge of many things. Come and share your master's happiness!"

The man with the two talents also came. "Master," he said, "you entrusted me with two talents; see, I have gained two more."

His master replied, "Well done, good and faithful servant! You have been faithful with a few things; I will put you in charge of many things. Come and share your master's happiness!"

Then the man who had received the one talent came. "Master," he said, "I knew that you are a hard man, harvesting where you have not sown and gathering where you have not scattered seed. So I was afraid and went out and hid your talent in the ground. See, here is what belongs to you."

His master replied, "You wicked, lazy servant! So you knew that I harvest where I have not sown and gather where I have not scattered seed? Well then, you should have put my money on deposit with the bankers, so that when I returned I would have received it back with interest.

"Take the talent from him and give it to the one who has the ten talents. For everyone who has will be given more, and he will have an abundance. Whoever does not have, even what he has will be taken from him. And throw that worthless servant outside, into the darkness, where there will be weeping and gnashing of teeth."

Note the transition in the parable. The servants are asked to steward earthly possessions. But the stewardship (their earthly training) serves to prepare them for stewardship in eternity. *Earthly stewardship is serious business, because its purpose is to prepare us for eternal ruling and reigning.*

Biblical prosperity is "the talents." It is merely the training tool the Lord uses to prepare us to be *put in charge of many things*.

The Lord's primary purpose for training us in biblical prosperity is to conform us to the character of Christ so that we can rule with Him for all eternity. So how do we become Christlike stewards? By understanding this spiritual principle: Godly stewardship is held in a perfect balance between holy Scripture and the Holy Spirit.

Let me give you an example. I have no mechanical ability. None. If I had attended a high school where shop classes were required, I would have entered adulthood severely maimed. So it was with great reluctance that I recently attempted to replace a simple part on our swimming pool pump. First, I got out the instruction manual and pored over it. Diagrams and instructions that, I am sure, would make perfect sense to most people served only to confuse me. Then I saw the 800 help number at the bottom of the instruction booklet. I knew that 800 number represented someone I could call on, someone I could trust and depend upon to guide me through my task. So, with the instruction manual in one hand and a portable phone in the other, I was able to accomplish the task.

The Lord has given us the Bible and the Holy Spirit. The Bible is our instruction manual, and the Holy Spirit is our "help," to whom we can call for perfect truth. We can depend on Him to guide us and to help us accomplish the tasks we are called to in life. The perfect principles of godly stewardship will always be revealed in Scripture and confirmed by the Holy Spirit.

There are over two thousand verses in Scripture that deal with financial matters. Over two-thirds of the parables deal with finances and stewardship. Each of those verses and parables represents a spiritual principle to guide us. The Lord uses the material realm to teach us about the spiritual realm, the natural to teach us about the supernatural.

Let me offer a word of warning. As stated above, godly steward-ship is held in a delicate balance between Scripture and the Holy Spirit's leading. This place of balance is what I call being in the mid-dle of the *river of God*. You must diligently seek to stay in the middle of the river. Some people will get too *scriptural* and become legalis-tic and religious. When the river turns, they are washed up on the bank. The Pharisees followed the letter of the law, but not the spirit, and missed the anointed Son of God. Others get too *spiritual* and start to find hidden messages from God in everything they encounter. They too are in danger of being washed up on the shore, while the river flows on without them. If we study God's Word *and* discern gen-uine Holy Spirit instruction, we will stay in the middle of the river of God and fulfill His purpose for our lives.

Chapters 5 through 16 of this book explain how we can achieve this balance between Holy Scripture principles and Holy Spirit prompting so that we can remain in the middle of the river of God.

Scripture warns us that it is *the little foxes that spoil the vines* (see Song of Solomon 2:15 KJV). Chapters 5 through 14 will discuss ten of these *little foxes*. When I say little it should not be understood to mean unimportant; rather, I am referring to the *subtle* violations of **scriptural** principles that creep into our lives and hurt our steward-ship. These ten scriptural principles of stewardship are those that I most often see Christians violating. Avoiding or correcting these problems will guide you in your journey on the road to biblical pros-perity. Scriptural principles will help you develop godly stewardship now, in the Kingdom of God; more importantly, they will help you *store up eternal treasure in Heaven.*

Chapter 15 will discuss the importance of our relationship with the Holy Spirit. Chapter 16 will give examples of great men of the Bible who were able to master the balance between the written Word of God and being led by the Holy Spirit.

BIBLICAL BASICS

1. Biblical prosperity has three components: godly success, godly affluence and influence, and godly freedom.

2. A simple test to see if you are on the road to biblical prosperity is to look at your life and determine whether it is yielding the *fruit of the Spirit.*

3. Biblical prosperity is the ongoing result of godly stewardship.

4. Godly stewardship is held in a perfect balance between what Scripture and the Holy Spirit tell us about managing those things the Lord has entrusted into our care.

5. In order to develop godly stewardship in each of us, the Lord uses the material realm to teach us about the spiritual realm and the natural to teach us about the supernatural.

6. The true purpose of stewardship is to glorify God and to prepare us to rule and reign with Christ for eternity.

Catch for us the foxes, the little foxes that ruin the vineyards.

Song of Solomon 2:15a

IT ALL BEGINS WITH TITHES AND OFFERINGS

"The Keys to Supernatural Release"

No eye has seen, no ear has heard, no mind has conceived what God has prepared for those who love Him.

1 Corinthians 2:9b

People probably ask me more questions about tithes and offerings than about any other biblical subject. Sadly, the subject often comes up when I am counseling with a couple who are hopelessly in debt.

I ask, "Are you tithing?"

They look at me like I have just thrown a box of snakes at their feet and respond, "No, how can we tithe? We can't even pay our bills!"

Let me try to explain this important concept. Tithing is an issue of trust and obedience. You can trust that the Lord will meet your needs as you obey Him. Scripture clearly teaches this principle: *If you insist on taking what God did not give to you, God will take back something that He did give to you.*

Consider the Garden of Eden. The Lord gave Adam and Eve the entire garden, but forbade them one tree. Adam and Eve took from that one tree and the Lord took the whole garden back from them.

The Lord rejected Saul as king of Israel, because Saul defied God and chose to touch the forbidden plunder from the conquest of King Agag.

> *"The Lord anointed you king over Israel. And He sent you on a mission and told you, 'Go and completely destroy the sinners, the Amalekites, until they are all dead.' Why haven't you obeyed the Lord? Why did you rush for the plunder and do exactly what the Lord said not to do?"*
>
> *"But I did obey the Lord, "Saul insisted. "I carried out the mission He gave me. I brought back King Agag, but I destroyed everyone else. Then my troops brought in the best of the sheep and cattle and plunder to sacrifice to the Lord your God in Gilgal."*
>
> *But Samuel replied, "What is more pleasing to the Lord: your burnt offerings and sacrifices or your obedience to His voice? Obedience is far better than sacrifice. Listening to Him is much better than offering the fat of rams. Rebellion is as bad as the sin of witchcraft, and stubbornness is as bad as worshiping idols. So because you have rejected the word of the Lord, He has rejected you from being king."*
>
> 1 Samuel 15:17-23

Saul knew he had disobeyed God and was now trying to justify it. As a result, the Lord chose David to be king. Everything that the Lord had given Saul He now took away from him and gave to David.

The Book of Malachi tells us that to take the Lord's tithes and offerings is to rob Him. Many believers fail to recognize that the consequences of robbing God affect us both in the Kingdom of God, on earth, and in the Kingdom of Heaven—robbing us of blessings and influence here and heavenly treasures that He had intended for us.

Yet, tithes and offerings continue to be one of the most difficult principles of stewardship for many believers to embrace. The simple truth is that tithes and offerings are not an option available to us when we have sufficient funds. They are the earthly manifestation of one of the Lord's most prevalent themes in Scripture, *the spiritual principle of sowing and reaping.*

It is difficult for our minds to comprehend that we gain by giving, that we grow by giving, and that being able to give is itself a gift from the Lord. This principle is so important to the Lord that He goes into great detail regarding tithes and offerings. First, He commands us to give; then He instructs us regarding a proper heart attitude when we give; and finally, He reveals the blessings promised to a joyful giver.

The command is found, among other places, in Leviticus 27:30, "A tithe of everything from the Lord, whether grain from the soil or fruit from the trees, belongs to the Lord; *it is holy to the Lord.*" This is not merely an Old Testament principle. In the Gospel of Luke, Jesus rebukes the Pharisees for their lack of compassion but confirms the command to tithe, "Woe to you Pharisees, because you give God a tenth of your mint, rue and all other kinds of garden herbs, but you neglect justice and the love of God. You should have practiced the latter *without leaving the former undone*" (Lk. 11:42).

The apostle Paul tells us that we can expect to reap to the degree that we have sown; he admonishes us to give with a right heart attitude.

> *Remember this: Whoever* **sows sparingly** *will also* **reap sparingly***, and whoever* **sows generously** *will also* **reap generously***. Each man should give what he has decided in his heart to give, not reluctantly or under compulsion,* **for God loves a cheerful giver***. And God is able to make all grace*

abound to you, so that in all things at all times, having all that
you need, you will abound in every good work.

2 Corinthians 9:6-8

Finally, we discover the blessings promised to the joyful giver. One
of my favorites is Luke 6:38, "Give and it will be given to you. A good
measure, pressed down, shaken together and running over, will be
poured into your lap. For with the measure you use, it will be meas-
ured to you." Please, I beg you not to ignore this powerful foundational principle of stewardship.

I could pour secular financial wisdom into you forever, but— if
you choose to ignore Scripture's principles regarding tithes, offerings,
and giving to the poor—your purse will still have holes in it and your
life will be without biblical prosperity. It is no coincidence that I have
never spoken to a believer, faithful with his tithes and offerings, who
was leading a joyless or fruitless life. Whenever you sow your treasure, time, or talents into the Kingdom of God, you will always reap a
supernatural harvest in due season.

This principle is beautifully illustrated in the books of Haggai and
Malachi. In the Book of Haggai, the Lord is taking the Israelites to
task for being so concerned about building their own houses that they
were not rebuilding the temple. Sternly, He warns them:

Now this is what the Lord Almighty says: "Give careful
thought to your ways. You have planted much, but have har-
vested little. You eat, but never have enough. You drink, but
never have your fill. You put on clothes, but are not warm.
You earn wages, only to put them in a purse with holes in it.

This is what the Lord Almighty says: "Give careful thought to
your ways. Go up into the mountains and bring down timber
and build the house, so that I may take pleasure in it and be
honored," says the Lord. "You expected much, but see, it

*turned out to be little. What you brought home, I blew away.
"Why?" declares the Lord Almighty. "Because of my house,
which remains a ruin, **while each of you is busy with his
own house**. Therefore, because of you the heavens have withheld their dew and the earth its crops. I called for a drought
on the fields and the mountains, on the grain, the new wine,
the oil and whatever the ground produces, on men and cattle,
and on the labor of your hands.*

Haggai 1:5-11

This curse of Haggai stands in stark contrast to the wonderful
blessings promised to the faithful giver in the Book of Malachi:

*"Bring the whole tithe into the storehouse, that there may be
food in My house. Test Me in this," says the Lord Almighty,
"and see if I will not throw open the floodgates of heaven and
pour out so much blessing that you will not have room enough
for it".*

Malachi 3:10-11

Four words in this Scripture absolutely amaze me: "Test Me in
this." Can you imagine? The Creator of the universe is telling us—the
dust that He breathed life into—that He wants to bless us so much
that He will let us test Him in the area of giving. If we do that, He will
be faithful to pour out a blessing that we cannot contain.

In the final analysis, when it comes to tithes and offerings the
question is simple. We all must ask ourselves, "Haggai or Malachi,
which "I" am I?"

BIBLICAL BASICS

1. Tithes and offerings are the foundation to biblical prosperity and godly stewardship.

2. The Lord commands us to tithe. Tithe means one-tenth. To tithe is to give ten percent of your gross income. To give less than ten percent is not a tithe; it is an offering. An offering can not replace a tithe.

3. The Lord instructs us as to the attitude of our hearts when we give: we must be cheerful givers.

4. The faithful giver of tithes and offerings should expect to reap an abundant harvest.

5. Obeying God's command to give tithes and offerings is a key that releases supernatural blessings in your life.

— 6 —

Beware of Debt

"Devilish Distraction"

A man is a slave to whatever has mastered him.

2 Peter 2:19

I can almost see the crush of oppression, like a heavy weight, on the shoulders of those I counsel regarding debt problems. Their faces are drawn; their souls are tormented with anxiety, fear, and depression; their eyes reflect a spirit of hopelessness. Without a doubt, I counsel more people whose lives have been savaged by credit abuse and mounting debt than by any other financial problem.

Make no mistake, "The borrower is servant to the lender" (Prov. 22:7b).

I am convinced that in this country satan's greatest spiritual weapon is *fear*. One of his greatest natural weapons is *debt*. Debt lures and tempts, consumes and crushes. It not only separates you from the money the Lord has entrusted to you, but can also separate you from your spouse, family, and—worst of all—a relationship with a loving God. It is a monster with many tentacles that wrap around us, pulling us under to a place where the pressure is so great we feel we cannot breathe. I have often seen the joyless faces of couples hopelessly in debt. I can feel the strain in the relationship between husband and wife, between parents and their children. What is worse, the financial *troubles of this world* prevent them from producing the fruit that God has called them to produce.

Excessive debt can cause eternal tragedy.

Listen to the cry of Nehemiah:

We have had to borrow money to pay the king's tax on our fields and vineyards. Although we are of the same flesh and blood as our countrymen and though our sons are as good as theirs, yet we have to subject our sons and daughters to slavery. Some of our daughters have already been enslaved, but we are powerless, because our fields and our vineyards belong to others.

Nehemiah 5:4-5

Then listen to the advice of Jesus through Paul, "Let no debt remain outstanding, except the continuing debt to love one another" (Rom. 13:8a).

However long it takes, today is the day to commit to becoming debt free.

You may respond, "But you don't know my situation. You don't know the hopeless mess that I have gotten myself into." You are right, I don't. I do know that we serve an awesome God who says, "Is anything too hard for the Lord?" (Gen. 18:14)

The Lord's plan, from the very beginning, has always been:

The Lord your God will bless you as He has promised, and you will lend to many nations but will borrow from none. You will rule over many nations but none will rule over you.

Deuteronomy 15:6

and,

72

*"I know the plans I have for you," declares the Lord, "plans
to prosper you and not to harm you, plans to give you hope
and a future."*

Jeremiah 29:11

I want to make a very important distinction between your *short-term debts* and your *long-term debts*. Long-term debts are usually associated with an underlying asset. For instance, when you buy a house you usually have a mortgage. When you buy a car you will usually have a long-term car note. Taking on long-term debt is generally not where most people get themselves into financial trouble. In a worst-case scenario you can sell the underlying asset and pay off the long-term debt.

It is generally short-term debt that destroys most people's finances. Short-term debt is any debt that *should* be paid off in less than 24 months and generally has no asset associated with it. Short-term debt usually consists of credit card debt, unsecured credit union loans, consolidation loans, and home equity loans that are spent on items other than the home. Short-term loans are usually associated with our *wants* rather than our *needs*. Short-term loans are spent on consumables such as clothes, travel, entertainment, and other non-essentials. The problem is that this debt remains long after the item purchased is consumed.

In my book *Money Came by the House the Other Day* (InSync Press, 2001), I give detailed instructions on how to identify and solve your debt problems. For the purposes of this book I will outline some of the basic steps:

A. Know the signs of too much short-term debt

1. You never have enough money at the end of the month to pay all of your bills.

2. You have nothing saved for emergencies.

3. You charge items to delay having to pay for them.

4. You make consolidation loans to pay off credit cards.

5. You "roll" credit card balances from one credit card to another.

B. Know how to attack the short-term debt problem

1. Confess your mess. Prayerfully admit to the Lord, with a broken and contrite spirit, that you have been a poor steward of what He has entrusted to you.

2. Repent, which means change direction. Turn from your poor stewardship and ask the Lord to take charge of your finances.

3. Literally lay all of your debts before Him in prayer. If you are married, it is important that the whole family participate in this prayer.

4. Destroy all of your credit cards.

5. Develop a written plan to get out of debt. Scripture tells us to write down the vision. Post it where you will see it every day and pray over it daily.

6. Prepare a personal balance sheet to track your debts at the end of each month. Graph your debts so you will see progress as they decline.

7. Pay cash. Your spending decisions are less impulsive when you pay with cash instead of a charge card.

8. As you commit yourself to godly stewardship of your finances, expect the supernatural to happen. Expect funds from unexpected sources. Expect raises and better jobs. I cannot tell you how many times I have seen the Lord supernaturally intervene on someone's behalf once they began to travel the road of godly stewardship.

9. Speak the positive vision, not the negative. We serve, "the God who gives life to the dead and calls things that are not as though they were" (Rom. 4:17).

The Best News Yet

The above list is helpful in the natural, but this truth transcends all: Our God is a debt cancelling God. His nature is to forgive and set free.

What did you do to have your sin debt cancelled? Nothing but believe. If He did that for your sin debt, He can do that for your financial debt as well. And, He can do it in an instant. Only believe!

BIBLICAL BASICS

1. One of satan's most vicious weapons is to subtly lure us into overwhelming debt, thereby robbing us of our peace, joy, and relationships.

2. Only by submitting our finances to the Lord and becoming godly stewards will we ever find a way out of the burden of debt.

3. You must develop a written plan to get out of debt and submit that plan to the Lord.

4. Expect the Lord to intervene once He has seen that you are committed to becoming a godly steward, regardless of the short-term cost you may have to pay.

5. It has always been the Lord's plan that His people "will lend to many nations but will borrow from none."

6. Have faith for the miracle. God is no respecter of persons; He responds to faith, not unbelief.

— 7 —

Seek Godly Wisdom

"He Still Answers All"

Get wisdom, get understanding; do not forget my words or swerve from them. Do not forsake wisdom, and she will protect you; love her and she will watch over you. Wisdom is supreme; therefore get wisdom.

Proverbs 4:5-7a

Would you like to be "exalted?" Would you like to be "honored?" Scripture tells us that the man who embraces wisdom (Christ) will receive these gifts. Unfortunately, the opposite is true. If you want to rapidly lose ground, depend on your own reasoning and thinking.

Recently a young businessman came into my office and began to tell me about a business he had just purchased. As he talked, my suspicions grew. I asked him if he had consulted with an attorney or CPA before purchasing the business. He told me that he had not, that he had relied on what the seller and the seller's attorney told him about the business. As we continued to talk it became apparent that it was not *what he had been told*, but *what he had **not** been told* that was about to become a very costly lesson for him. This man, who knew very little about the business he had just bought, plowed ahead because it all sounded so good. The result was that he had agreed to assume a quarter of a million dollars of debt that he had no idea even existed. Here was a very bright, highly educated individual who made a very costly mistake simply because he failed to walk in wisdom. Scripture warns us,

The first to present his case seems right, till another comes forward and questions him.

Proverbs 18:17

There is a way that seems right to a man, but in the end it leads to death.

Proverbs 14:12

Trust in the Lord with all your heart and lean not on your own understanding; in all your ways acknowledge Him, and He will make your paths straight.

Proverbs 3:5-6

The Bible tells us that our natural mind constantly wars against the word of God. The natural mind wants its way, its plan; and it wants it now. Left uncontrolled, it will seek out an environment and people who will confirm the correctness of its wants.

For everything in the world—the cravings of sinful man, the lust of his eyes and the boasting of what he has and does— comes not from the Father but from the world. The world and its desires pass away, but the man who does the will of God lives forever.

1 John 2:16-17

The spiritual man will always seek the mind of Christ about everything.

We must discipline our thought life, or our natural mind will keep us out of the Kingdom of God, and there will be no biblical prosperity in our lives. If we constantly seek the mind of Christ, the Lord will release His supernatural wisdom upon us.

For though we live in the world, we do not wage war as the world does. The weapons we fight with are not the weapons of the world. On the contrary, they have divine power to demolish strongholds. We demolish arguments and every pretension that sets itself up against the knowledge of God, and we take captive every thought to make it obedient to Christ.

2 Corinthians 10:3-5

Virtually everyone I talk to admits that they were not prepared to take on the responsibilities of financial stewardship. Yet, we are personally and professionally faced with a lifetime of questions regarding investments, insurance, retirement, debt, educational costs, etc. There are men and women who spend their whole lives trying to develop expertise in just one of these areas, yet most people must deal with all of them to some degree throughout their lifetime. What do you do? How do you begin to seek godly wisdom? Here are three suggestions:

1. *Heed the warning of the prophet Hosea,* "My people [say you and me] are destroyed from lack of knowledge" (Hos. 4:6).

Accept the fact that you will be struggling with stewardship issues all of your life and begin to seek financial wisdom now. You will find many excellent books on Christian financial planning at your local Christian bookstore. Buy several and continually refer to them.

2. *Very cautiously and very carefully begin to surround yourself with wise counselors.* Scripture tells us, "Plans fail for lack of counsel, but with many advisers they succeed" (Prov. 15:22).

In the Body of Christ are many who can provide you with counsel. Ask the Lord to bless you with men and women who possess godly wisdom and influence, who will help to provide you with counsel in matters of stewardship.

3. *Remember that every question you encounter regarding stewardship is answered in Scripture.* There are no new questions, Ecclesiastes 1:9 reminds us, "What has been will be again, what has been done will be done again; there is nothing new under the sun."

Seek the Lord for supernatural wisdom and He will provide it.

Ask and it will be given to you; seek and you will find; knock and the door will be opened to you. For everyone who asks receives; he who seeks finds; and to him who knocks, the door will be opened.

Matthew 7:7-8

For instance, a non-believer may ask you to join with him in a business venture that holds great promise for profit. However, if you test this proposal against Scripture, you will find a warning, "Do not be yoked together with unbelievers" (2 Cor. 6:14a). Note that it was not necessary for you to fully understand the particular business venture in order to understand what you should do.

The Lord will always supernaturally reveal His counsel in these matters to those who diligently seek Him.

BIBLICAL BASICS

1. Wisdom is supreme; that is why the Lord gave us the Book of Proverbs. Read a chapter a day.

2. When you are faced with a financial decision, resist the temptation to do as the world does. Seek wisdom from Scripture, the Holy Spirit, and wise counselors. Your answer will come when all three of these sources align and confirm one another. You will recognize it by the peace that you have.

— 8 —

BE DILIGENT ABOUT THE BASICS

"Knowing the Condition of Your Flocks"

Be sure you know the condition of your flocks, give careful attention to your herds.

Proverbs 27:23

Whenever I counsel with a couple, I begin by asking some basic questions in order to determine their financial situation. Often the conversation will go something like this:

"What is the value of all of your assets?"

"I don't know."

"How much debt do you have?"

"Well, I'm not exactly sure, but it is a lot."

"How much do you earn?" This they can usually answer.

"How much do you spend?" To this question I almost always get the same answer, "More than I earn." And so it goes.

Most people having financial difficulties truly do not know how they got there. And it is understandable, since most people have never been instructed on even the most basic principles of personal financial management and stewardship.

However, Scripture forbids us from simply drifting through life with our finances in chaos. God is a God of order, not confusion. The Lord doesn't *suggest* that we know the conditions of our flocks; He commands it. That means that we must obtain a basic understanding of what we *own* and what we *owe* (a personal balance sheet) and what we *earn* and what we *spend* (a personal income statement).

There are many excellent Christian books on financial planning that will teach you to prepare these basic financial statements. These books will instruct you on how to use your personal financial statements to identify strengths and weaknesses, to take corrective action against past problems, and to set the appropriate goals of a good steward.

Remember, "A prudent man sees danger and takes refuge, but the simple keep going and suffer for it" (Prov. 22:3).

THE JONES FAMILY
BALANCE SHEET
DECEMBER 31, 20XX

ASSETS		LIABILITIES & NET WORTH	
CURRENT ASSETS		**CURRENT LIABILITIES**	
Cash	$2,000	Credit Card Debt	$2,500
Bank Savings Account	6,000	Finance Company Loan	0
Stock Mutual Funds	8,000		
		TOTAL CURRENT LIABILITIES	
TOTAL CURRENT ASSETS	**16,000**		
		LONG TERM DEBTS	
FIXED ASSETS		First Mortgage	118,000
Residence	200,000	Second Mortgage	0
Automobiles	25,000	Auto Loans	20,000
Furniture, Fixtures &		Loan From Parents	0
Personal Effects	30,000		
		TOTAL LONG TERM DEBTS	**138,000**
TOTAL FIXED ASSETS	**255,000**		
		TOTAL LIABILITIES	**140,500**
OTHER ASSETS			
Life Insurance Cash	0		
Surrender Value	2,000		
401 (K) Plan	30,000		
Pension Plan	14,000		
		NET WORTH	**174,500**
TOTAL OTHER ASSETS	**44,000**		
		TOTAL LIABILITIES &	
TOTAL ASSETS	**$315,000**	**NET WORTH**	**$315,000**

ILLUSTRATION 1

YOUR FAMILY
BALANCE SHEET
DECEMBER 31, 20XX

ASSETS		LIABILITIES & NET WORTH	
CURRENT ASSETS		**CURRENT LIABILITIES**	
Cash	_____	Credit Card Debt	_____
Bank Savings Account	_____	Finance Company Loan	_____
Stock Mutual Funds	_____		
TOTAL CURRENT ASSETS	_____	**TOTAL CURRENT LIABILITIES**	_____
FIXED ASSETS		**LONG TERM DEBTS**	
Residence	_____	First Mortgage	_____
Automobiles	_____	Second Mortgage	_____
Furniture, Fixtures &		Auto Loans	_____
Personal Effects	_____	Loan From Parents	_____
Boat	_____		
		TOTAL LONG TERM DEBTS	_____
TOTAL FIXED ASSETS	_____	**TOTAL LIABILITIES**	_____
OTHER ASSETS			
Life Insurance Cash	_____		
Surrender Value	_____		
401 (K) Plan	_____		
Pension Plan	_____	**NET WORTH**	_____
TOTAL OTHER ASSETS	_____	**TOTAL LIABILITIES &**	
		NET WORTH	_____
TOTAL ASSETS	_____		

ILLUSTRATION 2

THE JONES FAMILY
INCOME STATEMENT
FOR THE MONTH ENDING

	Jan	Feb	Mar	Apr	May...
INCOME:					
Salary Husband	$3,500				
Salary Wife	3,000				
Interest & Dividends	<u>100</u>				
TOTAL INCOME	**6,600**				
MANDATORY EXPENSES					
Tithes & Offerings	(800)				
Taxes	(1,075)				
Savings	(500)				
LIVING EXPENSES					
First Mortgage	(1,000)				
Home Repair & Maintenance	(50)				
Automobile Payments	(800)				
Auto Insurance, Gas, Repairs, Etc.	(200)				
Food	(500)				
Clothing	(150)				
Gas, Electricity, Water	(150)				
Homeowners Insurance & Taxes	(150)				
Medical & Dental	(50)				
Telephone	(75)				
Life Insurance	(50)				
Vacations	(200)				
Education	(100)				
Health & Beauty Care	(45)				
Misc. Expenses	(100)				
Entertainment	(150)				
Credit Card Payments	(250)				
Second Mortgage	0				
Finance Company Loan	0				
Other	0				
Other	0				
TOTAL EXPENSES	**(6,395)**				
NET GAIN OR (LOSS) EACH MONTH	**$205**				

ILLUSTRATION 3

THE JONES FAMILY
INCOME STATEMENT
FOR THE MONTH ENDING

	Jan	Feb	Mar	Apr	May...

INCOME:
Salary Husband _____
Salary Wife _____
Interest & Dividends _____

TOTAL INCOME _____

MANDATORY EXPENSES
Tithes & Offerings _____
Taxes _____
Savings _____

LIVING EXPENSES
First Mortgage _____
Home Repair & Maintenance _____
Automobile Payments _____
Auto Insurance, Gas, Repairs, Etc. _____
Food _____
Clothing _____
Gas, Electricity, Water _____
Homeowners Insurance & Taxes _____
Medical & Dental _____
Telephone _____
Life Insurance _____
Vacations _____
Education _____
Health & Beauty Care _____
Misc. Expenses _____
Entertainment _____
Credit Card Payments _____
Second Mortgage _____
Finance Company Loan _____
Parents Loan _____
Other _____
Other _____
_____

TOTAL EXPENSES _____

NET GAIN OR (LOSS) EACH MONTH _____

ILLUSTRATION 4

BIBLICAL BASICS

1. The Lord requires that we understand the condition of our finances.

2. The basic tools for understanding our financial condition are a personal balance sheet and income statement.

3. Use these basic tools. They will enable you to identify financial problems and to set goals to correct them.

— 9 —

DIVERSIFY

"Apples and Baskets"

Give portions to seven, yes to eight, for you do not know what disaster may come upon the land.

Ecclesiastes 11:2

I could sum up this chapter in two words: *stock market*.

Just a few short years ago, people couldn't own enough stock. They invested every penny they had in the stock market; and when they ran out of funds, they borrowed money to invest in the stock market. For a short season it was exciting and wonderful to watch their "paper wealth" climb to the heavens.

Then came the crash. Savings were wiped out, pensions destroyed, and as their paper wealth quickly melted away, it left in its wake a mountain of disillusionment and debt.

I could tell you about the "I thought it was such a good deal" tales that I so often hear. Almost always they reveal a story of someone who invested far too much of what they owned into a single type of investment, only to have that investment collapse.

Once again, Scripture *commands* that we diversify. It is never wise to put everything into one stock, one bank, one business venture, one loan, or one of anything.

As good stewards, we should strive to gain knowledge about the various financial decisions we will face during the seasons of our life such as:

1. Cash/emergency fund management;

2. Buying stocks and mutual funds;

3. Buying bonds and other fixed income investments;

4. Purchasing real estate (usually buying your home);

5. Purchasing various types of insurance;

6. Purchasing annuities;

7. Preparing for the high cost of higher education for our children;

8. Preparing for retirement;

As I have said, there are several good financial planning books available at your local Christian bookstore. Prepare yourself with the knowledge you will need in order to take care of what the Lord has entrusted to you. Properly allocate it into portions of seven or eight.

Solomon, the richest man who ever lived, knew this secret. So should we.

Sow your seed in the morning, and at evening let not your hands be idle, for you do not know which will succeed, whether this or that, or whether both will do equally well.

Ecclesiastes 11:6

BIBLICAL BASICS

1. Never invest a substantial portion of what you own in a single investment.

2. Diversification of what you own is a command from the Lord, not a request.

3. It is our responsibility to learn how to properly diversify our assets.

4. Never invest in anything that you do not thoroughly understand.

— 10 —

AVOID THE SCHEMES AND DREAMS OF MAN

"But It Sounded So Good"

You will be approached. Well-meaning, and not-so-well-meaning friends, family, and strangers will come to you with "great ideas" and potential investments. Their proposals will sound good, because Scripture says, *"The first to present his case seems right, till another comes forward and questions him"* (Prov. 18:17).

I cannot count the number of people that I counseled with, *after* they had listened to the counsel of the unwise or the ungodly. From grape farms in South America, to rare coins, to shaky multi-level businesses, to "penny" stocks, to baseless business ventures, they all violated the same common scriptural principles. Because people wanted to make a lot of money quickly, they either did not seek wise counsel or ignored it, if it wasn't what they wanted to hear; they excluded the Lord from the process; and they acted hastily. Finally, just when I thought I'd seen it all, along comes the Internet, offering the same scams. People can't wait to embrace these ideas just because "they're on the Internet."

Here are just a few of the many Scriptures that speak to this important principle:

He who walks with the wise grows wise, but a companion of fools suffers harm.

Proverbs 13:20

Dishonest money dwindles away, **but he who gathers money little by little makes it grow.**

Proverbs 13:11

Do not be misled: "Bad company corrupts good character."

1 Corinthians 15:33

There is a way that seems right to a man, but in the end it leads to death.

Proverbs 14:12

Many are the plans in a man's heart, but it is the Lord's purpose that prevails.

Proverbs 19:21

Do you know what type of scam cheats people out of the most money every year? Religious scams. That is correct; con artists know that because "religious people" have good hearts they are easy targets. Never invest or give money to someone just because they share your race, religion, occupation, church membership, club or school membership, etc.

Too many people fall victim to schemes and dreams because they do not have the ability to say no. They often knowingly make unwise choices in order to avoid hurting someone's feelings. We must learn to be God pleasers and not people pleasers. If you are rejected for saying no, take comfort in the fact that no one was more rejected for doing the right thing than Jesus. Be bold enough to say no, shake the dust from your feet, and move on.

It might be helpful, when making a financial decision, to remember that the funds you foolishly give away or misspend are not yours. They have been entrusted to you by the Lord for your wise use. Every spending decision we make should be viewed in this light.

Let no one deceive you with empty words, for because of such things God's wrath comes on those who are disobedient. Therefore do not be partners with them.

Ephesians 5:6-7

For everyone looks out for his own interest, not those of Jesus Christ.

Philippians 2:21

...there will be false teachers among you....In their greed these teachers will exploit you with stories they have made up....Bold and arrogant, [they] are not afraid to slander celestial beings....For they mouth empty, boastful words and, by appealing to the lustful desires of sinful human nature, they entice people..."

2 Peter 2:1,3,10,18

BIBLICAL BASICS

1. It's not a question of if, but when, you will be approached by someone whom the enemy will try to use to separate you from what the Lord has entrusted you to manage.

2. Don't invest with someone just because they share your race, religion, occupation, club membership, or some other common interest. Some of the most popular scams around are religious scams.

3. Learn to say no and to not fear the rejection of man.

4. Develop godly discernment. If your decisions are made in the light of biblical principles with Holy Spirit guidance, you will be able to avoid the schemes and dreams of man.

Provide for the Future

"So Noah, Why the Big Boat?"

*...The race is not to the swift or the battle to the strong, nor does food come to the wise or wealth to the brilliant or favor to the learned; **but time and chance happen to them all.***

Ecclesiastes 9:11

Every so often I hear the argument that it is unscriptural to plan for the future. The argument goes something like, "Well, I'm just going to trust the Lord." Sounds holy, doesn't it? The only problem is that it's nonsense. We are stewards. We are called to survey all that the Lord has entrusted to us and to provide the best possible care of it that we can.

For instance, one of the most precious gifts the Lord entrusts to us is our family. To not provide for their future is to violate your position as their covering and steward to them.

If anyone does not provide for his relatives, and especially for his immediate family, he has denied the faith and is worse than an unbeliever.

1Timothy 5:8

Each of you should look not only to your own interests, but to the interests of others.

Philippians 2:4

Scripture actually says that we *are not to worry or be anxious about the future*. In fact, the very first book of the Bible tells two wonderful stories about a couple of God's servants who are preparing for the future. Both Noah and Joseph understood that the time to store up provision is *before* disaster strikes.

It is interesting to see that the Lord refers to those who refuse to provide for the future as "sluggards" and warns us of their future.

*Go to the ant, you sluggard; consider its ways and be wise! It has no commander, no overseer or ruler, **yet it stores provisions** in summer and gathers its food at harvest.*

Proverbs 6:6-8

A sluggard does not plow in season; so at harvest time he looks but finds nothing.

Proverbs 20:4

The sluggard buries his hand in the dish; he is too lazy to bring it back to his mouth. The sluggard is wiser in his own eyes than seven men who answer discreetly.

Proverbs 26:15-16

It is our responsibility to gain the financial wisdom necessary to determine our needs for things such as insurance, the educational expenses of our children, and retirement. To not do so would be the equivalent of Noah's saying, "Hmm, looks like it's starting to rain; better get busy on that boat."

THE JONES FAMILY
EMERGENCY FUND CALCULATION

INCOME STATEMENT		EMERGENCY FUND NEEDS
INCOME:		
Salary Husband	$3,500	
Salary Wife	3,000	
Intrest & Dividends	100	
TOTAL INCOME	**6,600**	0
MANDATORY EXPENSES		
Tithes & Offerings	(800)	
Taxes	(1,075)	
Savings	(500)	
GROUP "B" EXPENSES		
First Mortgage	(1,000)	1,000
Home Repair & Maintenance	(50)	50
Automobile Payments	(800)	800
Auto Insurance, Gas, Repairs, Etc.	(200)	200
Food	(500)	500
Clothing	(150)	
Gas, Electricity, Water	(150)	150
Homeowners Insurance & Taxes	(150)	150
Medical & Dental	(50)	50
Telephone	(75)	75
Life Isurance	(50)	
Vacations	(200)	
Education	(100)	100
Health & Beauty Care	(45)	
Misc. Expenses	(100)	100
Entertainment	(150)	
Credit Card Payments	(250)	
Second Mortgage	0	
Finance Company Loan	0	
Other	0	
Other	0	
TOTAL EXPENSES	**(6,395)**	**$3,175**
NET GAIN OR (LOSS) EACH MONTH	**$205**	
TOTAL EMERGENCY FUND EQUALS 12 TO 18 MONTHS OF NEEDS:		**$38,100 TO $57,150**

ILLUSTRATION 5

99

BIBLICAL BASICS

1. Providing for the future needs of your family is biblical.

2. In the Book of Genesis the Lord provides us with two excellent stories about planning for the future—Noah and Joseph.

3. The Lord chastises those who do not plan for the future and refers to them as *sluggards*.

4. The time to plan for the future is now.

— 12 —

FIND SOMEONE TO WHOM YOU WILL BE ACCOUNTABLE

"We All Need Covering"

For I myself am a man under authority, with soldiers under me. I tell this one, "Go" and he goes; and that one, "Come," and he comes. I say to my servant, "Do this," and he does it.

Matthew 8:9

Before I get too deep into this chapter I want to clarify one extremely important point. No man, no one, should ever stand between you and your relationship with the Holy Spirit, your covering. The relationship is direct, and will *never* require an intermediary. Scripture is clear that the Holy Spirit, as our covering, will provide us with all the wisdom we need.

But you have an anointing from the Holy One, and all of you know the truth. As for you, the anointing you received from Him remains in you, and you do not need anyone to teach you. But as His anointing teaches you about all things and as that anointing is real, not counterfeit—just as it has taught you, remain in Him.

1 John 2:20,27

With that understanding we should seek to find a godly mentor who will aid us in becoming increasingly more accountable to the

Holy Spirit. Joshua had Moses, Elisha had Elijah, and David had Nathan. It is the Lord's plan that iron sharpen iron. Prayerfully seek the Lord to lead you to someone whose godly character and integrity are beyond reproach, someone who can be trusted to counsel and advise you periodically with your personal financial situation. Reveal your strengths and weaknesses and set long and short-term goals that you can jointly monitor and pray for.

Therefore confess your sins to each other and pray for each other so that you may be healed. The prayer of a righteous man is powerful and effective.

James 5:16

In addition to a godly mentor, you should share your financial decisions with your spouse. I usually see one of two problems between husbands and wives when it comes to stewardship of the family's finances.

The first problem occurs when the husband makes all the financial decisions without consulting his wife. While it is true that the husband covers the wife and heads the household, it is also true that God has given him a spouse to make him whole. Without her intuitive nature and sense of discernment, the stewardship decisions a husband makes will not receive their full anointing—because he is using only one-tenth of the potential power that the Lord has made available.

How could one man chase a thousand, or two put ten thousand to flight?

Deuteronomy 32:30a

The other problem I see is the husband totally withdrawing himself from the family's finances, expecting the wife to handle everything. This method also violates scriptural principles, and the Lord will not release His blessing upon a violated principle. Husbands, you are the head of the household; therefore, you will be held accountable for the stewardship of everything that the Lord has entrusted to your family. It is your scriptural duty to be actively involved in the management of your family's finances.

BIBLICAL BASICS

1. God is a God of order, and as such He has intended that we should mentor one another.

2. Prayerfully seek the Lord to reveal His intended choice of a mentor for you. Do not move into that relationship until you and, if you are married, your spouse, have a peace and agreement about who it should be.

3. Husbands and wives should steward their finances jointly. God has appointed the husband as the authority and the covering over the wife; however, if the two of you are not in agreement on a financial decision, seek the Lord and do not let strife into your decisions. Remember satan knows that the power of two in agreement is ten times the power against him.

4. Be careful—even well-intentioned mentors can be influenced by their own flesh or even demons. If you sense that the relationship is shifting from mentoring to control or bondage, break it off.

LIVE A LIFE OF CHARACTER, DISCIPLINE, AND HONESTY

"What Would Jesus Do?"

Be imitators of God....

Ephesians 5:1a

My son, do not make light of the Lord's discipline, and do not lose heart when He rebukes you, because the Lord disciplines those He loves, and He punishes everyone He accepts as a son.

Hebrews 12:5b-6

So many of our financial struggles would not exist if we had the character to make the right decision regardless of the personal cost, the discipline to say no, and the honesty to confess our sins.

We need to be God pleasers, seeking the mind of Christ in all that we do, and not waste our time seeking the fickle approval of man.

How are we transformed into the character of Christ? The answer may seem trite, but it is by asking the question, What would Jesus do in this situation? and then doing it.

Do not merely listen to the word, and so deceive yourselves. Do what it says.

James 1:22

We must remember that every stewardship decision we make will be revealed to us again in the light of the perfect judgment of Christ. Therefore, we need to live our lives as if all of our financial decisions were reported on the nightly news and our checkbook was printed in the daily newspaper.

> *Do not be deceived: God cannot be mocked. A man reaps what he sows. The one who sows to please his sinful nature, from that nature will reap destruction; the one who sows to please the Spirit, from the Spirit will reap eternal life. Let us not become weary in doing good, for at the proper time we will reap a harvest if we do not give up. Therefore, as we have opportunity, let us do good to all people, especially to those who belong to the family of believers.*

Galatians 6:7-10

> *...make every effort to add to your faith goodness; and to goodness, knowledge; and to knowledge, self-control; and to self-control, perseverance; and to perseverance, godliness; and to godliness, brotherly kindness; and to brotherly kindness, love. For if you possess these qualities in increasing measure, they will keep you from being ineffective and unproductive in your knowledge of our Lord Jesus Christ....For if you do these things, you will never fall, and you will receive a rich welcome into the eternal kingdom of our Lord and Savior Jesus Christ.*

2 Peter 1:5-8,10-11

BIBLICAL BASICS

1. Our stewardship decisions should reflect a life of Christlike character, discipline, and honesty.

2. All of our decisions will be revealed to us again at the judgment seat of Christ, and rewards will be handed out accordingly.

3. The testing of your integrity in the natural will determine your supernatural seat in eternity.

— 14 —

EMBRACE GREAT EXPLOITS

"Impossible, Difficult, Done"

The people who know their God shall be strong, and carry out great exploits.

Daniel 11:32b NKJ

When I called, You answered me; You made me bold and stouthearted.

Psalm 138:3

I can do everything through Him who gives me strength.

Philippians 4:13

God's people think too small. The Lord has not called you to spend your life worrying about your finances. If you are in His will, the promise is clear that He will supply all of your needs. Your focus should be on boldly carrying out His plan for your life and on performing great exploits in His name.

However, we must remember that the Lord's economy is different from ours. His approach is always *impossible, difficult, done*. When the task at hand seems impossible, rejoice—He is about to stretch your faith. Faith is the key, because it releases the supernatural into our lives. Very seldom will the Lord allow *great exploits* to unfold in your life the way you would have planned them.

Every great man in the Bible faced the impossible. David killed a giant and routed a nation with five smooth stones. Samson destroyed one thousand Philistines with the jawbone of an ass. Gideon defeated the entire Midianite army with three hundred men armed with trumpets and jars of clay. With a cane and a brother, Moses set three million people free. Joshua conquered a nation by obediently marching around a fortress. Jesus had a cross and a promise and brought salvation to the world.

But, here is the catch…to perform supernatural exploits you must be constantly focused on that *still small voice*. I am often troubled by Isaiah 43:18-19a:

Forget the former things.…See, I am doing a new thing! Now
it springs up; do you not perceive it?

You see, I think we can become so distracted by the things of this world that when the Lord presents us with a supernatural opportunity, we miss it because we didn't perceive it. We need to be constantly listening with our spirits for Holy Spirit direction, *expecting* that when we do hear from Him, *it will* be an unusual or impossible request. His ways will always be higher than our ways. The Lord will never ask you to do what you can do in your own strength. That would cause pride and not bring glory to Him. He will ask you to do the impossible. Be ready.

After wandering with the people in the desert for 40 years, Joshua faced what appeared to be an impossible task. He was to take a land inhabited by "giants." When we face our giants, we should be comforted by the words of the Lord to Joshua. The Lord does not change; His words still apply to us today.

Now then, you and all these people, get ready to cross the
Jordan River into the land I am about to give to them—to the
Israelites. I will give you every place where you set your foot,

as I promised Moses....No one will be able to stand up against you all the days of your life. As I was with Moses, so I will be with you; I will never leave you nor forsake you. Be strong and courageous, because you will lead these people to inherit the land I swore to their forefathers to give them. Be strong and very courageous....Do not let this Book of the Law depart from your mouth; meditate on it day and night, so that you may be careful to do everything written in it. Then you will be prosperous and successful.

Joshua 1:2-3, 5-8

BIBLICAL BASICS

1. We are called to embrace great exploits.

2. Satan will try to distract us from those exploits with financial bondages.

3. The Lord's calling upon us will at first always look *impossible*, then *difficult*, then *done*.

4. God will always provide the supernatural means to accomplish what He has called us to do—if we provide integrity, obedience, and faith.

5. Uncommon success comes when uncommon action gets uncommon anointing.

6. Godly determination is revealed by your unbroken focus.

7. It's not what you know or don't know; it's not what you have or don't have; it's knowing that He is all you need.

I have much more to say to you, more than you can now bear. But when He, the Spirit of Truth, comes, He will guide you into all truth. He will not speak on His own; He will speak only what He hears, and He will tell you what is yet to come. He will bring glory to Me by taking from what is Mine and making it known to you. All that belongs to the Father is Mine. That is why I said the Spirit will take from what is Mine and make it known to you.

John 16:12-15

— 15 —

WONDERFUL COUNSELOR

"The Holy Spirit"

In Chapter 4 we said: Godly stewardship is held in a perfect balance between holy Scripture and the Holy Spirit.

In the last ten chapters we discussed ten *scriptural* principles that are vital to godly stewardship. We discussed the importance of His Word, the Bible, to answer our every question with its inerrant truth, its rich depth, and abundant wisdom.

What other book can you read for a lifetime, and have it speak to you in a fresh and exciting way every time you pick it up? Its endless layers of richness bring peace and guidance to the soul and discernment to the spirit.

It *is* the *living* Word of God. And, what brings *life* to the *word* is the Holy Spirit.

In this chapter we will discuss how our relationship with the Holy Spirit is the important other half of the balance necessary for godly stewardship.

As we read and study the Bible, the living word is revealed to us by progressive revelation from the Holy Spirit.

Using His Word, the Holy Spirit guides and counsels us. He steadies and comforts our hearts, as He continually reminds us that He is with us and whispers, "Fear not." Through Scripture the Holy Spirit reveals the heartfelt comfort of Psalms, the wisdom of Proverbs, and the knee-bending hope of eternal salvation proclaimed in the Gospels. The Holy Spirit is able to continually mature us in Christ using "the sword of the Spirit, which is the word of God" (Eph. 6:17b). The Holy Spirit and His Word cannot be separated.

I will tell you that this is a difficult and humbling chapter to write. It would be foolish for anyone to try to describe the fullness of the Holy Spirit. If ever there was a subject that "we see but a poor reflection as in a mirror" (1 Cor. 13:12), it would be the Holy Spirit.

Scripture provides us with the principles of stewardship. Then as we seek the Holy Spirit, He breathes life into these principles and imparts them into our spirits—where we are literally changed to think as He does.

It is like sitting at a magnificent banquet table. The food looks delicious and smells wonderful, but it will only bring life to our bodies if we eat it. We must feast on the Word of God daily, seeking personal revelation from the Holy Spirit. As we do our part, the Holy Spirit will use His Word to bring new *life* to our soul and spirit.

It is from this precious *revelation presence* of the Holy Spirit that true stewardship and biblical prosperity are born.

Let me give you an example from Scripture of how important the presence of the Holy Spirit is to us. Few people would argue with the statement that King David was one of the greatest kings of biblical times, and that God dearly loved him. But Scripture tells us that to look at David, you would never have known that he was destined for greatness. In fact, when Samuel was sent by the Lord to anoint one of Jesse's sons as the new king of Israel, he picked the wrong son. The Lord had to instruct him,

> *Do not consider his appearance or his height, for I have rejected him. The Lord does not look at the things man looks*

*at. Man looks at the outward appearance, but the Lord looks
at the heart.*

1 Samuel 16:7

Having been corrected,

*Samuel took the horn of oil and anointed him in the presence
of his brothers, and from that day on **the Spirit of the Lord
came upon David** in power.*

1 Samuel 16:13a

Now, fast forward. David has been a mighty king for many years.
He has all the trappings of success: palaces, wives, servants, armies,
and wealth. And David sins. Broken and repentant, he turns to the
Lord for forgiveness. Knowing that sin brings consequences, David
begs the Lord for mercy. David's primary concern is not to retain his
kingship or his wealth; he doesn't even ask the Lord to spare his life.
His one request is, *"Do not cast me from Your presence or take Your
Holy Spirit from me"* (Ps. 51:11).

David knew what must be central to every believer's life. Every
good thing in the Kingdom of God and the Kingdom of Heaven will
flow from our relationship with the Holy Spirit. One simple sentence
from the prophet Zechariah says it all: " *'Not by might nor by power,
but by My Spirit,' says the Lord Almighty"* (Zech. 4:6).

So who is this precious Holy Spirit?

He Is a Person

Benny Hinn says it well in his book *Good Morning, Holy Spirit*:

*The Holy Spirit is a person. And just like you, He can feel,
perceive, and respond. He gets hurt. He has the ability to love
and the ability to hate. He speaks, and He has His own will.
But exactly who is He? The Holy Spirit is the Spirit of God*

117

the Father and the Spirit of God the Son. He is the power of the Godhead—the power of the Trinity.

Perhaps the greatest revelation of the charismatic movement is that we can have a progressively deeper and deeper relationship with the Holy Spirit, right here and right now. As a parent longs for intimate relationship with his child, so does the Holy Spirit long for and offer us the gift of intimate relationship with Him. The most precious moments of my life are when His presence is so heavy upon me that all I can do is lie on the floor and praise Him. Never doubt that the Holy Spirit is calling you to intimate fellowship with Him all the days of your life. It is God's will that we "be filled with the Spirit" (Eph. 5:18b).

His Presence Is a Gift From God the Father

And afterward, I will pour out My Spirit on all people.

Joel 2:28a

And I will put My Spirit in you and move you to follow my decrees and be careful to keep My laws.

Ezekiel 36:27

I will pour out My Spirit on your offspring, and My blessing on your descendants.

Isaiah 44:3b

His Presence Is a Gift From Jesus

But I tell you the truth: It is for your good that I am going away. Unless I go away, the Counselor will not come to you; but if I go, I will send Him to you.

John 16:7

Don't you know that you yourselves are God's temple and that
God's Spirit lives in you?

1 Corinthians 3:16

The Nature of the Holy Spirit

The purpose of this chapter is to discuss the biblical traits and characteristics of the Holy Spirit that will guide us into mature stewardship and biblical prosperity as He develops the character of Christ in us.

1. The Holy Spirit is the Spirit of truth.

But when He, the Spirit of truth, comes, He will guide you into all truth. He will not speak on His own; He will speak only what He hears, and He will tell you what is yet to come. He will bring glory to Me by taking from what is Mine and making it known to you.

John 16:13-15

The enemy of deception is truth. The antidote to the *deception of wealth* is the *Spirit of truth*.

We live in the age of "situational ethics." A non-hearing, non-seeing society has taken nice sounding words such as *tolerance, acceptance, non-judgmental,* and *inclusive* and used them to convincingly gray the pure white-hot truth of God. The "truth" has become like a box of building blocks. We pull out whatever pieces we need to construct a pretty building to house our success and lifestyle and call that building truth. Debt? It's the American way. Tither? Don't be so judgmental. Lack of integrity and character? It's just business; everybody does it. The problem is, of course, that a wooden block house cannot stand in the storm. If you ignore the voice of the Holy Spirit long enough, eventually you will be like the foolish builder:

> *But everyone who hears these words of Mine and does not put them into practice is like a foolish man who built his house on sand. The rain came down, the streams rose, and the winds blew and beat against that house, and it fell with a great crash.*
>
> Matthew 7:26-27

> *Do not be deceived: God cannot be mocked. A man reaps what he sows. The one who sows to please his sinful nature, from that nature will reap destruction; the one who sows to please the Spirit, from the Spirit will reap eternal life.*
>
> Galatians 6:7-8

However, the believer should never worry about the storm, because we have a promise—that the Holy Spirit who lives in us will guide us into truth.

> *...the Spirit of truth. The world cannot accept Him, because it neither sees Him nor knows Him. But you know Him, for He lives with you and will be in you.*
>
> John 14:17

How do we recognize the Spirit of truth speaking to us? Generally, He will reveal truth to us in one of five ways:

A small still voice (see 1 Kings 19:12);

A prompting in our conscience (see Rom. 2:15);

A confirmation of His Word (see Ps. 25:14);

A "check" in our spirit (see Rom. 8:16);

A sense of peace (see Jn. 16:32-33).

Does the Holy Spirit still speak to us today? Absolutely!

How often? Daily, if we seek Him with all of our heart and all of our spirit.

Think about it. Do you think that you, as a loving parent, will ever reach a point in your life when you say to your children, "Well, I have spoken to you long enough. I've told you everything that you need to know. I have no plans to speak with you any longer. I will now become totally mute"? Of course not! How much more does our perfect Father long to communicate with His children? The Holy Spirit is there waiting to provide us with the truth for all of our questions.

2. The Holy Spirit is the Spirit of counsel.

But I tell you the truth: It is for your good that I am going away. Unless I go away, the Counselor will not come to you; but if I go, I will send Him to you.

John 16:7

What if you came to me with a financial problem and I pointed you toward two rooms? In one room were the most brilliant attorneys, CPAs, financial planners, stockbrokers, investment bankers, and businessmen in the world. In the other room was the Holy Spirit. Which room would you choose to enter to seek the answer to your problem?

The choice seems so clear. The Holy Spirit is *omnipotent*, all powerful. He is *omniscient*, all knowing. He is *omnipresent*, able to be in all places at all times. What better counsel could there be? Yet, we have been taught to depend on our own minds and to seek the wisdom of the world for answers. It is only when worldly counsel fails us that we cry out, "Oh God, help me!

Scripture commands us to do the exact opposite:

Dear friends, do not believe every spirit, but test the spirits to see whether they are from God, because many false prophets have gone out into the world. This is how you can recognize the Spirit of God: Every spirit that acknowledges that Jesus Christ has come in the flesh is from God, but every spirit that does not acknowledge Jesus is not from God....

You, dear children, are from God and have overcome them, because the one who is in you is greater than the one who is in the world. They are from the world and therefore speak from the viewpoint of the world, and the world listens to them. We are from God, and whoever knows God listens to us; but whoever is not from God does not listen to us.

1 John 4:1-6a

The man without the Spirit does not accept the things that come from the Spirit of God, for they are foolishness to him, and he cannot understand them, because they are spiritually discerned.

1 Corinthians 2:14

3. The Holy Spirit is the Spirit of wisdom and understanding.

*The Spirit of the Lord will rest on him—**the Spirit of wisdom and of understanding**, the Spirit of counsel and of power, the Spirit of knowledge and of the fear of the Lord.*

Isaiah 11:2

*We have not received the spirit of the world but the Spirit who is from God, **that we may understand** what God has freely given us. This is what we speak, not in words taught us by human wisdom but in words taught by the Spirit.*

1 Corinthians 2:12-13a

There is a supernatural anointing that will bless your stewardship decisions if you lay them at the feet of the Lord and ask the Holy Spirit to guide you. But, be forewarned, He may not always give you the answer you are seeking.

For the wisdom of this world is foolishness in God's sight.

1 Corinthians 3:19a

Let's revisit an example I used earlier. Suppose you are approached by a non-believer to join him in a business venture that holds great promise for profit. You take it to the Holy Spirit and He tells you no, "Do not be yoked together with unbelievers" (2 Cor. 6:14).

Notice that the Holy Spirit never spoke to whether the venture would be profitable or not, as human wisdom approaches would do. The Holy Spirit was concerned with the mixing of light and darkness.

It is usually at this point that people will convince themselves they did not hear from the Holy Spirit or that "that isn't what that Scripture meant."

If you can resist this temptation to quench the Holy Spirit, He will supernaturally reveal His wisdom and understanding on all matters. The result will be far more than you could have asked for or imagined:

We do, however, speak a message of wisdom among the mature, but not the wisdom of this age or of the rulers of this age, who are coming to nothing. No, we speak of God's secret wisdom, a wisdom that has been hidden and that God destined for our glory before time began. None of the rulers of this age understood it, for if they had, they would not have crucified the Lord of glory. However, as it is written: "No eye has seen, no ear has heard, no mind has conceived what God

123

has prepared for those who love Him"—but God has revealed it to us by His Spirit.

1 Corinthians 2:6-10a

4. The Holy Spirit is the Spirit of power.

*But you will receive **power** when the Holy Spirit comes on you.*

Acts 1:8a

*For God did not give us a spirit of timidity, but a **spirit of power**, of love and of self-discipline.*

2 Timothy 1:7

There are two ways to succeed: by striving in the *flesh* or with the *Lord's favor*. Success in the flesh often exacts a high price and ends at the grave. Success through the favor of the Holy Spirit brings peace and comes with eternal rewards.

Every person of character and integrity in the Bible knew that his or her success was a result of the power of the Lord.

Zechariah heard from the Lord, " *'Not by might nor by power, but by My Spirit,' says the Lord Almighty"* (Zech. 4:6b). Paul confirms it in the New Testament:

My message and my preaching were not with wise and persuasive words, but with a demonstration of the Spirit's power, so that your faith might not rest on men's wisdom, but on God's power.

1 Corinthians 2:4-5

5. *The Holy Spirit reveals the mind of Christ.*

And we, who with unveiled faces all reflect the Lord's glory,
are being transformed into His likeness *with ever-increas-*
ing glory, which comes from the Lord, who is the Spirit.

2 Corinthians 3:18

May I ask you a few questions? If you were rich, what would you
do with your life? How would you spend your time? How would your
relationships change? What would you focus your time, talents, and
treasures upon?

Now, let me ask you one more question. If you were rich and had
the perfect mind of Christ, what would you do with your life? Are the
answers to the first scenario the same as the answers to the second?
They should be.

The Holy Spirit reveals the mind of Christ to us. And it is the mind
of Christ that leads us into true stewardship. *This is how we find the*
Lord's perfect will for our lives.

But God has revealed it to us by His Spirit.

The Spirit searches all things, even the deep things of God.
For who among men knows the thoughts of a man except the
man's spirit within him? In the same way no one knows the
thoughts of God except the Spirit of God. We have not
received the spirit of the world but the Spirit who is from
God, that we may understand what God has freely given us.

1 Corinthians 2:10-12

We have a choice. We can reject the Holy Spirit's work in us and
attempt to define our own purpose for living. This path is a tragic mistake. Separation from the Holy Spirit and the Lord's will for your life
brings only emptiness, striving, failure, and regret. That is why

Scripture implores us, "Since we live by the Spirit, let us keep in step with the Spirit. Let us not become conceited, provoking and envying each other" (Gal. 5:25-26).

> *Do not conform any longer to the pattern of this world, but be transformed by the renewing of your mind. Then you will be able to test and approve what God's will is—His good, pleasing and perfect will.*

Romans 12:2

6. *The Holy Spirit is the Spirit of comfort and peace.*

> *And I will ask the Father and He will give you another Comforter (Counselor, Helper, Intercessor, Advocate, Strengthener and Standby) that He may remain with you forever.*

John 14:16 AMP

> *But the fruit of the Spirit is love, joy, peace, patience, kindness, goodness, faithfulness, gentleness and self-control.*

Galatians 5:22a

The road to biblical prosperity and godly stewardship is littered with our mistakes. Unwise purchases, bad investments, poor discernment, broken relationships, and the shoddy care of what has been entrusted to us are all common errors. We all look back with regrets.

The Lord has provided for this. It is the Holy Spirit who comforts us in the midst of our mistakes and then guides us into greater wisdom. As we confess and repent, He is always faithful to forgive.

Satan will be there to remind you of your mistakes and condemn you, but it is the Holy Spirit within, who constantly urges us to do as Paul did, "Forgetting what is behind and straining toward what is ahead, I press on toward the goal to win the prize for which God has called me heavenward in Christ Jesus" (Phil. 3:13b-14).

BIBLICAL BASICS

The purpose of the first 15 chapters of this book is to provide a framework to help keep you in the middle of *the river of God*, God's perfect will for your finances and His purposes for your life. It is important to keep a balance between scriptural instruction and Holy Spirit confirmation. I recommend the following approach:

1. When a stewardship question presents itself, diligently search Scripture for guidance and ask the Holy Spirit for revelation.

2. After you have found what you believe is the scriptural answer to your question, seek wise counsel from godly advisors and from your spouse, if you are married. Their counsel should align itself with Scripture. Based on what they tell you, you may find yourself going back to Scripture for additional wisdom and understanding.

3. Lay all of the Scriptures you have found and the counsel of your advisors at the feet of the Lord and seek the Holy Spirit for confirmation. Wait for confirmation and direction. The Holy Spirit will guide you into truth and wisdom if you will patiently wait on His voice.

You will know that you have the Lord's answer when all three steps are in agreement and *you are walking in peace over your decision.*

To the man who pleases him, God gives wisdom, knowledge and happiness, but to the sinner he gives the task of gathering and storing up wealth to hand it over to the one who pleases God.

Ecclesiastes 2:26a

16

A Prophet and a King

"Abraham and Solomon"

When it comes to biblical prosperity and godly stewardship, sometimes the best illustrations come from true stories. The purpose of this chapter is to study two great men of God whose lives are living illustrations of what we have discussed so far.

The lives of many individuals in Scripture serve as powerful examples of integrity, character, and stewardship. But two men are extraordinary examples of lives that typify the characteristics of godly stewardship that lead to true biblical prosperity: a prophet and a king— Abraham and Solomon. One gave birth to the nation of Israel, the other reigned over that nation during the height of its golden age. Their lives reveal the godly stewardship the Lord looks for and develops in us so that He can release His blessings of biblical prosperity upon us.

Abraham—the Faithful Overcomer

For he is a prophet, and he will pray for you and you will live.

Genesis 20:7b

I greatly admire Abraham. He seemed to continually stumble into and out of sin…but he loved the Lord, longed for His presence, and was *full of faith*. Abraham had the kind of faith that trusts a merciful

God who wants to wrap His arms around each of us and say, "I love you despite your flesh."

Biblical prosperity is impossible without faith.

Imagine that you are 75 years old. You are quietly sitting on your front porch, minding your own business, when suddenly you hear a voice. The voice tells you to leave your home, your family, and your relatives—and move to a land that you've never seen before. What's more, the voice continues, if you do this,

> *I will make you into a great nation and I will bless you; I will make your name great, and you will be a blessing. I will bless those who bless you, and whoever curses you I will curse; and all peoples on earth will be blessed through you.*
>
> Genesis 12:2-3

What would you do? How would you respond to the voice? You see, I don't think the voice thundered at Abraham. I think the voice whispered to him.

I believe it is that same voice of the Lord that still speaks to us today. Sadly, it is too often drowned out by the concerns, worries, and fears of the day.

Weak faith deafens us to the gentle whisper of a calling Lord.

That is why it is important to study Abraham's reaction to the voice of the Lord. Before answering God, Abraham did not list the advantages and disadvantages of being obedient to the voice of the Lord. He did not contact the Canaan Chamber of Commerce to determine whether the local economy was strong. He did not check out the school systems, study the local crime statistics, or inquire about the cost of housing.

Scripture simply says, "So Abram left…" (Gen. 12: 4). And one of the results of his faithful response was, "Abram had become very wealthy in livestock and in silver and gold" (Gen. 13:2).

This was just the first of many illustrations of Abraham's life of faith. Genesis chapter 13 explains that not only had Abraham become wealthy, but also his wayward nephew Lot had become wealthy. Subsequently, a struggle developed between the two men's herdsmen over grazing land. To avoid conflict, Abraham made an offer to Lot:

Let's not have any quarreling between you and me, or between your herdsmen and mine, for we are brothers. Is not the whole land before you? Let's part company. If you go to the left, I'll go to the right; if you go to the right, I'll go to the left.

Genesis 13:8-9

Notice what happened.

*Lot looked up and saw that the whole plain of the Jordan was well watered, like the garden of the Lord, **like the land of Egypt**, toward Zoar. (This was before the Lord destroyed Sodom and Gomorrah.) So Lot chose for himself the whole plain of the Jordan and set out toward the east.*

Genesis 13:10-11a

Lot looked with the *eyes of the flesh*. He placed his trust in what he saw, and what he saw *looked like Egypt*. You know the rest of the story. We next see Lot, a man who had great wealth, running to escape the divine destruction of Sodom and Gomorrah with only the clothes on his back. Trusting in what *appeared right* cost him all of his possessions, his sons-in-law and even his wife.

Contrast this with Abraham's approach: "You go east, I'll go west; you go west, I'll go east." Abraham looked upon the situation with *eyes of faith.* The decision was unimportant to him, *because he had faith that the favor of the Lord was upon him; therefore, he would prosper in any circumstance. He trusted the Lord to care for him and to direct his path.*

Without faith there is no biblical prosperity.

There may be temporary financial success, but don't confuse fleeting seasons of "having" with eternal biblical prosperity. Faith is where we take a stand. Faith is where we confess that what we cannot see is supreme and that what we cannot touch rules our life.

Now faith is being sure of what we hope for and certain of what we do not see.

Hebrews 11:1

It is at the altar of faith that we say, "I believe the miraculous can be a daily experience," and begin to understand,

Without faith it is impossible to please God, because anyone who comes to Him must believe that He exists and that He rewards those who earnestly seek Him.

Hebrews 11:6

What kind of faith brings biblical prosperity? Bold faith.

By faith *Abraham, when called to go to a place he would later receive as his inheritance, obeyed and went, even though he did not know where he was going. By faith he made his home in the promised land....For he was looking forward to the city with foundations, whose architect and builder is God.*

Hebrews 11:8-10

This was a faith that Paul still marveled at thousands of years later as he spoke about Abraham.

Yet he did not waver *through unbelief regarding the promise of God, but was strengthened in his faith and gave glory to God, being fully persuaded that God had power to do what He had promised.*

Romans 4:20-21

But, faith isn't the only characteristic of biblical prosperity that Abraham demonstrated.

Biblical prosperity is impossible without the willingness to separate.

This one hurts. As the Lord conforms us to the character of a godly steward, He will always ask us to separate from people or places in our life that He knows are not good for us. A study of Abraham's life reveals a succession of increasingly difficult separations. However, each request for separation is followed by a powerful promise of biblical prosperity. Abraham was asked to separate from:

1. His homeland
2. His nephew Lot
3. His son Ishmael
4. His son Isaac

We first encounter Abraham living in Haran. It is interesting to note how Abraham got there.

Terah took his son Abram, his grandson Lot son of Haran, and his daughter-in-law Sarai, the wife of his son Abram, and together they set out from Ur of the Chaldeans to go to **Canaan**. *But when they came to Haran, they settled there.*

Genesis 11:31

Apparently, the Lord had already instructed Abraham's (Abram's) father to go to Canaan, but for some reason he became distracted; or

135

he compromised along the way and settled for Haran. Having ignored the gentle voice of the Lord, he died there. However, as soon as Abraham's father was dead, the Lord said to Abraham, "…'Leave your country, your people and your father's household and go to the land I will show you' " (Gen. 12:1). With the requirement of separation came the promise of blessing.

> *I will make you into a great nation and I will bless you; I will make your name great, and you will be a blessing. I will bless those who bless you, and whoever curses you I will curse; and all peoples on earth will be blessed through you.*

> Genesis 12:2-3

Next, the Lord required Abraham to separate from Lot, although Lot was one of Abraham's closest relatives. As we have already said, Abraham's people and Lot's people were quarreling over the available grazing lands. Immediately, when Abraham had complied with the Lord's request,

> *The Lord said to Abram after Lot had parted from him, "Lift up your eyes from where you are and look north and south, east and west. All the land that you see I will give to you and your offspring forever. I will make your offspring like the dust of the earth, so that if anyone could count the dust, then your offspring could be counted. Go, walk through the length and breadth of the land, for I am giving it to you."*

> Genesis 13:14-17

The third required separation was even more painful. Ishmael was Abraham's firstborn son, but he was a stumbling block to the Lord's eternal purpose for Isaac. The Lord required Abraham to separate from Ishmael. With that separation came a great promise, "…because it is through Isaac that your offspring will be reckoned" (Gen. 21:12).

Once again, Abraham was obedient to the Lord. But his tests were not over. If fact, the fourth test is almost impossible to imagine. The Lord required Abraham not only to separate from his son Isaac, but also to literally sacrifice him.

> *Then God said, "Take your son, your only son, Isaac, whom you love, and go to the region of Moriah. Sacrifice him there as a burnt offering on one of the mountains I will tell you about."*

Genesis 22:2

Scripture tells us that Abraham had faith to believe that even if he killed his son, the Lord would raise Isaac up again. Regardless, this had to be one of the most difficult days of recorded biblical history. Surely, as Abraham ascended that mountain a devastating pain was crushing his heart. But he was faithful to the Lord's final request for separation. As he was about to carry out the Lord's instruction, an angel of the Lord stopped him with this promise,

> *I swear by Myself, declares the Lord, that because you have done this and have not withheld your son, your only son, I will surely bless you and make your descendants as numerous as the stars in the sky and as the sand on the seashore. Your descendants will take possession of the cities of their enemies, and through your offspring all nations on earth will be blessed, because you have obeyed Me.*

Genesis 22:16-18

From Abraham's willingness to make the ultimate sacrifice came the seed of Christ. Where would we be today if Abraham had refused the Lord's request?

Is there something the Lord is asking you to separate yourself from? As we move down the road of biblical prosperity, one requirement is sure; the Lord will continually point out the *Lots* and the *Ishmaels* in our lives and ask us to separate from them. If we are obedient to His direction, His great promise will be released upon us.

Biblical prosperity is impossible without the Tithe.

Genesis chapters 12 and 14 tell an interesting story.

Abraham's nephew, Lot, is once again in trouble. Genesis chapter 14 relates that the kings of Sodom and Gomorrah are at war with several other kings. Having been defeated in battle, the cities of Sodom and Gomorrah are pillaged; and the enemy has carried away all of their goods, their people, and Abraham's nephew Lot.

When Abraham hears what has happened to his nephew, he assembles an army of only 318 men, pursues the captors and defeats an opposing army made up of four kingdoms! As Abraham returns home with Lot and his possessions and the spoils that had been taken from Sodom and Gomorrah, two very important events occur.

First, Abraham is met by a high priest of God named Melchizedek. The entire meeting is described in one paragraph, but its importance rings down through the ages. Melchizedek brings bread and wine (the symbols of Christ) to Abraham, and Abraham gives Melchizedek a tithe of all of the spoils he has taken.

An eternal exchange has taken place. In order to understand the importance of this exchange, we need to go back to Genesis chapter 12.

I will make you into a great nation and I will bless you; I will make your name great, and you will be a blessing. I will bless those who bless you, and whoever curses you I will curse; and all peoples on earth will be blessed through you.

Genesis 12:2-3

This is a covenant promise from the Lord to Abraham, but at this point in time, it is only a *promise*. The Lord said, I *will* make you into a great nation, and I *will* make your name great, and I *will* bless those who bless you, etc. All of these promises are to take place at some future point in time.

However, as Abraham tithes (see Gen. 14) to the high priest and king Melchizedek, (a type and shadow of Christ) a supernatural prosperity *is released* upon him. The promise becomes manifested in Abraham's life. The tithe was the *covenant connection*—that is, the point of contact that connected the promises of God and manifested them into the actual blessings of God.

> *Then Melchizedek king of Salem brought out bread and wine. He was priest of God Most High, and he **blessed** Abram, saying, "**Blessed be** Abram by God Most High, Creator of heaven and earth. And **blessed be** God Most High, who delivered your enemies into your hand."*
>
> Genesis 14:18-20a

The "I will" had now become "the actual blessing;" the promise of the covenant was manifested by the tithe. *The tithe was the covenant connection.* It still is today, because "I the Lord do not change" (Mal. 3:6a).

The second important event was that Abraham understood the power of the covenant connection. After he had tithed, the thankful kings of Sodom and Gomorrah told Abram to keep the rest of the goods he had recovered, but to return their people. To this proposal Abraham replies,

> *I have raised my hand to the Lord, God Most High, Creator of heaven and earth, and have taken an oath that I will accept nothing belonging to you, not even a thread or the thong of a*

sandal, **so that you will never be able to say, 'I made Abram rich'.**"

Genesis 14:22b-23

Abraham knew that no man had the ability to prosper him. He knew better than to even give the appearance that his prosperity came from any source other than the Lord. He knew that as he gave unto the Lord, it would be given back unto him many times over.

Like Abraham, we must be willing to understand that the tithe is our covenant connection between the promises of the Lord and the manifestation of those promises in our lives.

Biblical prosperity is impossible without Obedience.

"God, You want him to kill his son?" I can still remember asking this question as a very young boy. I was the firstborn son in a Jewish family. I can tell you that as a youngster in Sunday school hearing the story of Abraham and Isaac brought me no comfort or encouragement. I didn't understand the Lord's purpose or Abraham's willingness. It was years later, reviewing it through the eyes of Christ, that I began to see its significance.

The Lord will test us, just as he tested His servant Abraham.

What is your Isaac? Is it your job, your family, your hobbies, your traditions, your prejudice? Whatever we cling to in the name of safety and security will also be a stumbling block between us and the Lord. As you mature in the Lord, He will require that you be willing to sacrifice it on the altar.

For Abraham, it was his only son. The son he had waited years for was now being required as a sacrificial lamb.

I remember thinking as a child, *How could he do that? What kind of monster could Abraham be?*

140

But I had only half of the story. I didn't have the New Testament.

*By faith Abraham, when God tested him, offered Isaac as a sacrifice. He who had received the promises was about to sacrifice his one and only son, even though God had said to him, "It is through Isaac that your offspring will be reckoned." **Abraham reasoned that God could raise the dead**, and figuratively speaking, he did receive Isaac back from death.*

Hebrews 11:17-19

There you have it, the rest of the story. Abraham's great obedience was born of his great faith. He was able to sacrifice his son, knowing that God would raise Isaac from the dead to establish a great nation as He had promised. Likewise, we can obediently sacrifice whatever the Lord asks of us, knowing that God showed His great love for us by sacrificing and raising from the dead His own Son, in order to establish an eternal kingdom where we can join Him forever.

You may ask, "What do these dramatic acts of faith and obedience have to do with biblical prosperity?" The answer is found immediately after the Lord released Abraham from having to sacrifice his son.

*I swear by Myself, declares the Lord, that because you have done this and have not withheld your son, your only son, I will surely bless you and make your descendants as numerous as the stars in the sky and as the sand on the seashore. Your descendants will take possession of the cities of their enemies, and through your offspring all nations on earth will be blessed, **because you have obeyed Me**.*

Genesis 22:16-18

Perhaps no other man in Scripture better illustrates the first four characteristics necessary for biblical prosperity than Abraham. Biblical prosperity will always be directly related to our ***faith, our***

141

willingness to separate, to tithe, and our obedience to the Lord's commands.

Solomon—the Surprise Request

Biblical prosperity is impossible without Wisdom and Knowledge.

Did you know that the Lord appeared to Solomon twice? Almost all of us are familiar with the famous first vision. Solomon is a new, untested king, and the Lord appears to him and instructs him to ask for whatever he wants.

Solomon replies, "Give me wisdom and knowledge, that I may lead this people, for who is able to govern this great people of Yours?" (2 Chron. 1:10)

The Lord, deeply moved by Solomon's request, responds,

> *Since this is your heart's desire and you have not asked for wealth, riches or honor, nor for the death of your enemies, and since you have not asked for a long life but for wisdom and knowledge to govern my people over whom I have made you king, therefore wisdom and knowledge will be given you. And I will also give you wealth, riches and honor, such as no king who was before you ever had and none after you will have.*

2 Chronicles 1:11-12

Solomon asked the Lord for wisdom and knowledge for the purpose of meeting the needs of God's people. The Lord saw a pure heart in Solomon and responded with an abundance of blessings on Solomon's life.

But there is more to Solomon's story.

Biblical prosperity is impossible without Humility.

In Second Chronicles chapter 7, we find Solomon the mature ruler. Blessed with wisdom and understanding, he has ruled well over a great nation. Among his many accomplishments, he has completed the temple of the Lord that his father David only dreamed of building. After Solomon dedicated the temple, the Lord appears to him once again, revealing the keys to biblical prosperity:

*If My people, who are called by My name, **will humble themselves and pray and seek My face and turn from their wicked ways**, then will I hear from heaven and will forgive their sin and will heal their land. Now My eyes will be open and My ears attentive to the prayers offered in this place.*

2 Chronicles 7:14-15

The fruit of Solomon's humility and prayer produced the golden age of Israel and, without his ever asking for it, the Lord granted him such great biblical prosperity that it is hard for us to grasp.

*King Solomon was greater in riches and wisdom than all the other kings of the earth. **All the kings of the earth sought audience with Solomon to hear the wisdom God had put in his heart.** Year after year, everyone who came brought a gift—articles of silver and gold, and robes, weapons and spices, and horses and mules.*

2 Chronicles 9:22-24

Biblical prosperity isn't found by seeking a raise or promotion. It doesn't come from picking good stocks, making good investments, or starting your own business. The road to biblical prosperity starts with "God's wisdom in your heart." It is a road that is humbly traveled on your knees. It is discovered in prayer and revealed by seeking the face of the Lord.

God opposes the proud but gives grace to the humble.

James 4:6

Wait a Minute!

You may be wondering, "Is this the same Solomon we read about in the second chapter of this book? What about all of his moaning in Ecclesiastes? What about all of those 'meaninglesses' he muttered? Is this the same King Solomon whom you are now using to illustrate biblical prosperity?"

Yes, it is the same Solomon, but

*As **Solomon** grew old, his wives **turned his heart after other gods, and his heart was not fully devoted to the Lord his God**, as the heart of David his father had been. He followed Ashtoreth the goddess of the Sidonians, and Molech the detestable god of the Ammonites. So Solomon did evil in the eyes of the Lord; he did not follow the Lord completely, as David his father had done....*

The Lord became angry with Solomon because his heart had turned away from the Lord, the God of Israel, who had appeared to him twice....So the Lord said to Solomon, "Since this is your attitude and you have not kept My covenant and My decrees, which I commanded you, I will most certainly tear the kingdom away from you and give it to one of your subordinates."

1 Kings 11:4-6,9,11

Biblical prosperity and godly stewardship are a way of life, and we can lose our way if we aren't ever vigilant.

So, now we have come full circle.

We are back where we started, asking the same questions we asked at the beginning of this book. Why the constant struggles with godly stewardship and biblical prosperity? Why struggle to master stewardship if we can lose it? Why seek biblical prosperity if we die and leave it all to someone else?

I am glad you asked.

Everything I have written so far serves only to lay a foundation. What we steward on earth *is* fleeting. Biblical prosperity on earth is left at the grave for others. The river of God moves on. It is only at the moment when we are absent from this body and present with the Lord that we understand it fully.

The purpose of godly stewardship and biblical prosperity in the final analysis is *to store treasure in Heaven.* When we stand before the Lord, an eternal treasure will await us. The sum of that treasure will be based on our acts of obedience here on earth. That is why we pursue biblical prosperity; that is why our goal is to be godly stewards; and that is what the remainder of this book is about.

The Lord has revealed to me that the last chapters of this book are the most important. I know that they will have an impact on your eternity.

BIBLICAL BASICS

1. Biblical prosperity is impossible without faith.

2. Biblical prosperity is impossible without the willingness to separate.

3. Biblical prosperity is impossible without the tithe.

4. Biblical prosperity is impossible without obedience.

5. Biblical prosperity is impossible without wisdom and knowledge.

6. Biblical prosperity is impossible without humility.

7. In an instant all of your biblical prosperity and acts of godly stewardship will be transformed into your eternal reward.

Part Two

THE KINGDOM OF HEAVEN

Treasures in Heaven

Behold, I am coming soon! My reward is with Me, and I will give to everyone according to what he has done.

Revelation 22:12

17

Pauper in Paradise

"What I Dread the Most"

I have a recurring fear.

I have died and gone to Heaven.

At first I am overwhelmed by the sheer magnitude of its beauty. Heaven's majesty is far, far more than I ever hoped or dreamed that it might be. The streets are brilliant gold, but barely noticed by those who walk them. The bejeweled buildings sparkle radiantly in a pure white light that is bright beyond description. There are no shadows, and no time passes. Everything reverberates with life, and the air is thick with a holy glory that envelops Heaven in eternal love.

But as I wander through Heaven I begin to notice that I can't find my house.

The glistening streets are bordered by beautiful mansions of every size and style. At the entrance to each house is a simple golden plaque with the owner's name inscribed upon it. Some I recognize. Paul's house can be seen from miles around. His next door neighbor, Moses, lives well too. The same street stretches on for miles and miles with the mansions of those we have never heard of. The martyrs, the missionaries, the unknown and the unsung all abide in homes that make the finest houses on earth seem like sharecropper shacks.

But I can't find my house among them and I am beginning to get a little concerned.

Then I see my pastor's house. It is every bit the mansion that I thought it would be. I walk up to it and knock on the door. It is open. There are no locks in Heaven. I don't see anyone, but I hear a television.

"Pastor, Pastor, is that you? It's me, Bob."

From the rear of the mansion I still recognize my shepherd's voice. "Bob, come on back, I'm in the den."

While he was on earth, one of the things my pastor loved to do was hunt. As I walk through the mansion toward the sound of his voice, I find myself in the midst of a magnificent great room. On the walls are hundreds of hunting trophies. The heads of every animal conceivable and some that I have never seen before stare down at me. Fifty-point bucks, lions, tigers, water buffalos all peer down with angelic faces.

As my pastor hugs me, he can't resist just one more pun. "I knew Heaven would be like this. I knew that the hunting would be out of this world. How are you, Bob? Glad to see you made it to Heaven."

I can't tell if he is surprised or not. He sits down on a zebra-patterned chair and resumes watching television.

"I'm well Pastor. But, once again, I am coming to you with a problem...I can't find my house. Pastor, what's that you're watching on television?"

"It's the hunting channel—all hunting, all day, everyday...it's heavenly."

"Oh, okay. Pastor, your home is beautiful, but...I can't find my house. Can you help me?"

"Can't find your house? Oh, yes, the Lord told me you'd come here asking about that. He said to give you this." From under his chair he pulls out a small bag and hands it to me. "The Lord said to give you this and to tell you that the rest would be explained to you later.

Would you like to sit down? There is a great bow hunting show coming on next."

"No, I'd better keep searching for my house. It was great seeing you again. I love what you've done with the place."

As I walk back through the house, I can see, by the decorating scheme, that my pastor's wife has not yet arrived in Heaven.

Totally confused, I walk out to the street and sit down on the curb, staring at the bag my pastor has given to me. It is a simple brown paper bag, like those that grocery stores sometimes use. It's very light and tied at the top by a single golden thread. As I loosen the thread and look inside, my heart sinks. The bag is full of ashes. I am not sure of the significance, but my sense of discernment tells me that this is not good.

"Bag full of ashes."

I look up. In front of me stands an angel. He is at least 12 feet tall, his hair so brilliantly golden that I have to turn away from its light. He is dressed in a radiant white robe, and at his side is a flaming sword. His blue eyes look down on me with a compassionate sadness as he repeats his statement.

"Bag full of ashes."

"Yes, but what does it mean?"

"It's your eternal reward."

"My reward! A bag full of ashes—what kind of reward is this?"

"It is the reward you earned on earth."

"No, it's not!"

"Yes, it is…and you were warned."

"No, I wasn't."

At this the angel steps back and holds out his arm. Golden letters appear on his robe:

If any man builds on this foundation using gold, silver, costly stones, wood, hay or straw, his work will be shown for what it is, because the Day will bring it to light. It will be revealed with fire, and the fire will test the quality of each man's work. If what he has built survives, he will receive his reward. If it is burned up, he will suffer loss; he himself will be saved, but only as one escaping through the flames.

1 Corinthians 3:12-15

"In that bag are the eternal remains of what you built on earth."

"But I wrote Christian books."

The angel turns toward me, and fire pours from his mouth. It envelops the bag in my hand and it too turns to ashes. "Did you write them to glorify the Lord or yourself?"

Jumping back, I can only blurt out, "But, but I preached and taught."

Once again, his breath is fire, and the single gold thread that was in my other hand is singed to cinders. "You loved standing in front of the people. You received your reward."

Desperately trying to plead my case, I sheepishly murmur, "But I counseled people at the church and I never charged them a fee."

I lift my arm up to protect myself from the fire that I know is coming. Instead the angel just shakes his head and begins to walk away.

I reach out to grab his robe and stop him. "That's it? My eternal reward is a bag full of ashes?"

He turns back to me one final time with fire blazing from his eyes. "Do you know the difference between the rich man in the Bible story of Lazarus, and you?"

I look down and shake my head no.

"The only difference is the blood of Christ."

Although his sword has never left his side, I feel like he has used it to cut me wide open.

"You both walked a life of indifference to the needs at your doorstep. You were spared the eternal torments of hell that he received, only because you accepted the saving blood of Christ. You were warned."

With that the angel walks away, leaving me sitting in a pile of ashes.

A pauper in paradise.

I fear being a pauper in paradise more than anything. I dread the thought of arriving in Heaven only to find out that I totally missed the purposes to which I was called on earth. To know the thousands of lives that I should have touched were never touched...and the lives they were to touch were never touched, and on and on.

The good news is that the prospect of being a "pauper in paradise" actually begins to answer some of our questions. The purposes of mastering biblical prosperity and godly stewardship come clearly into focus when we begin to see them not as a means of chasing temporary gain, but as God's plan for us to build upon an eternal foundation. Instead of being doubly deceived by the pursuit of wealth, we begin to understand that biblical prosperity is a means to being doubly blessed, both on earth and in Heaven.

When we have our financial house in order, it is no longer a stumbling block, distracting us from the Lord's purposes for our lives. Rather, we are free to receive all that He has prepared for us both in the Kingdom of God and the Kingdom of Heaven. We are commissioned to go and spread the gospel and be a light to a lost and dying world, all the while storing lasting treasures in Heaven.

It just doesn't get any better than that.

Command those who are rich in this present world not to be arrogant nor to put their hope in wealth, which is so uncertain, but to put their hope in God, who richly provides us with everything for our enjoyment. Command them to do good, to be rich in good deeds, and to be generous and willing to share. In this way they will lay up treasure for themselves as a firm foundation for the coming age, so that they may take hold of the life that is truly life.

1 Timothy 6:17-19

18

REAL MEAT BY-PRODUCTS

"The Meaning of Life"

I still remember vividly a series of television commercials for dog food from many years ago. Each commercial opened with a different dog eagerly bounding across the wide open spaces toward his feeding dish. These were beautiful animals. Their coats glistened, their eyes shined and their faces radiated in anticipation of being fed. As they honed in on their feeding dishes, their bodies literally shook with excitement.

As dogs ate, the announcer's voice explained why these canines were so happy and healthy. Unlike other dog foods, this dog food had *real meat by-products* in it; therefore, it was superior in every way to all other dog foods.

Real meat by-products! Can you imagine?

It sounds disgusting. Even as a child, I wondered what real meat by-products were; I sensed that real meat had to be better. I envisioned hoofs, horns, fat, and bone being ground up and stuffed into cans to be fed to these poor unsuspecting animals.

But the dogs didn't know any better. They were so eager, because they thought they were receiving the best. In truth, real meat by-products are the scraps that have been cut away to reveal the choicest cuts of meat. Next to the rock hard bone lies the tender T-bone, next to the tough gristle and fat you find the filet...but the dogs would never know it. So they dug into their counterfeit bounty, wolfing down everything that was set before them.

We can learn a truth from this illustration: *Prosperity on earth is **only** a **by-product** of godly stewardship, a mere shadow of what is to come in Heaven.*

Now, before you start gathering wood to burn me at the stake, let me explain. Yes, biblical prosperity is good. We need money to support ourselves and to spread the gospel message. Should we continue to persevere as good stewards of what the Lord has entrusted to us on earth? Certainly. However, it all must be viewed in light of Paul's warning to Timothy, "For we brought nothing into the world, and we can take nothing out of it" (1 Tim. 6:7).

Think about these few words. The best careers will all come to an end; and all talent ceases with the grave. At the end of the day, all of our possessions are forfeited to the next in line. Houses, cars, clothes, stocks, bonds, retirement accounts—all, as Solomon stated, turn out to be "meaningless." The truth is that our few years on earth are just a tiny crack in the sidewalk of eternity. On our death beds we won't be thinking about any of our material possessions.

*The **true product** of godly stewardship is **eternal treasure**.*

That is what it is all about. Searching for the meaning of life? Here it is:

Do not store up for yourselves treasures on earth, where moth and rust destroy, and where thieves break in and steal. But store up for yourselves treasures in heaven, where moth and rust do not destroy, and where thieves do not break in and steal. For where your treasure is, there your heart will be also.

Matthew 6:19-21

We Christians often become so focused on the here and now that we fail to step back and look at the eternal. The worries of this world attach themselves to us like tiny little anchors. One by one they weigh us down, to a point where all we can see is the world around us. Our perspective becomes distorted: the temporal *seems* like the eternal, and the eternal appears to be non-existent.

Yet Scripture tells us just the opposite. Throughout the Old and New Testaments we are instructed to lift our eyes above the horizon, to walk above the natural, to prepare ourselves daily for the supernatural. Moses knew it:

He regarded disgrace for the sake of Christ as of greater value than the treasures of Egypt, because he was looking ahead to his reward.

Hebrews 11:26

King David knew it. Even in the midst of his folly and sin he knew what was important, as he dropped to his knees and cried out,

One thing I ask of the Lord, this is what I seek: that I may dwell in the house of the Lord all the days of my life, to gaze upon the beauty of the Lord and to seek Him in His temple.

Psalm 27:4

Jesus Himself also knew it, and took great care to warn us,

The Son of Man is going to come in His Father's glory with His angels, and then He will reward each person **according to what he has done.**

Matthew 16:27

Look at those last six words: "according to what he has done."

You mean we have to do something? What about "not by works"? That's a good question, and it raises a very important point. Let's look at the entire verse:

For it is by grace you have been saved, through faith—and this not from yourselves, it is the gift of God—not by works, so that no one can boast. **For we are God's workmanship, created in Christ Jesus to do good works, which God prepared in advance for us to do.**

Ephesians 2:8-10

All the days ordained for me were written in Your book before one of them came to be.

Psalm 139:16b

Salvation is a gift from God to His children. It is accepting the blood of Christ plus nothing. However, once we are saved, there are specific works that the Lord has prepared for us to do since the beginning of time. *Our eternal reward will be directly related to how faithful we were in accomplishing the tasks He prepared for us to complete.*

This fact is so important, yet is seldom preached. The Bible speaks to this relationship between earthly works and eternal rewards over and over again. Here are several of the many Scriptures that encourage us to set our minds on things above (for a more complete listing, see Appendix):

The man who plants and the man who waters have one purpose, and each will be rewarded according to his own labor.

1 Corinthians 3:8

If any man builds on this foundation using gold, silver, costly stones, wood, hay or straw, his work will be shown for what it is, because the Day will bring it to light. It will be revealed with fire, and the fire will test the quality of each man's work. If what he has built survives, he will receive his reward. If it is burned up, he will suffer loss; he himself will be saved, but only as one escaping through the flames.

1 Corinthians 3:12-15

Serve wholeheartedly, as if you were serving the Lord, not men, because you know that the Lord will reward everyone for whatever good he does, whether he is slave or free.

Ephesians 6:7-8

Not that I have already obtained all this, or have already been made perfect, but I press on to take hold of that for which Christ Jesus took hold of me. Brothers, I do not consider myself yet to have taken hold of it. But one thing I do: Forgetting what is behind and straining toward what is ahead, I press on toward the goal to win the prize for which God has called me heavenward in Christ Jesus.

Philippians 3:12-14

Let us not become weary in doing good, for at the proper time we will reap a harvest if we do not give up.

Galatians 6:9

I am He who searches the hearts and minds, and I will repay each of you according to your deeds.

Revelation 2:23b

Behold, I am coming soon! My reward is with Me, and I will give to everyone according to what he has done.

Revelation 22:12

I believe the Lord's Word is clear. We are not called to be saved and then just do nothing. There is work for each of us to do. The Church has been commanded to take the gospel message to the world, *and each of us as a part of the Body of Christ has been assigned a role in that task from the beginning of time.*

We will be rewarded according to how well we answered the call on our lives. It is important that we don't compare ourselves with other Christians. You and I will be judged by the tasks we were specifically called to perform.

The road to biblical prosperity begins on earth, but it ends in Heaven.

BIBLICAL BASICS

1. Prosperity on earth is only a *by-product* of godly stewardship.

2. The true product of godly stewardship is eternal treasure stored in Heaven.

3. We will all stand before the judgment seat of Christ and be eternally rewarded, based on how well we accomplished the good works He prepared in advance for us to do.

4. He is coming soon, and His reward will be with Him.

...Stand at the crossroads and look; ask for the ancient paths, ask where the good way is, and walk in it, and you will find rest for your souls.

Jeremiah 6:16a

— 19 —

GRAVE CONSEQUENCES

"Chose Ye This Day"

I'll conclude with a true story.

It is an overcast, wintry New Orleans morning the week before Christmas 2000. I have just completed my first appointment of the day in an area known as the Westbank, and I am returning to my office. I have driven this road hundreds of times before. I know that there is a cemetery just a few hundred yards down the road.

As I approach the cemetery, a great stirring begins to come over me; I try to ignore it. I am sure that it is the Holy Spirit, but I don't want to talk about it. The stirring intensifies. An unseen force begins to gently turn my wrists, guiding my car into the graveyard. I pull over to a familiar parking place. Before I am even out of the car, my eyes have filled with tears. I know where I am.

I walk about 20 yards, and there at my feet is a small granite slab imbedded in the soil like a dirty gray bookmark. I know what it says. A name, a birth date, and a death date are the only remaining evidence that my father ever walked this earth. Even after 30 years, the tears still run down my face. A few feet to the left is more etched information, the same skeletal statistics for my sister.

And my heart cries out.

"Why Lord? Why have you brought me to this place?" I am screaming inside of myself.

"Why does a man with a wife and three children put a gun to his head and take his life? Why is the life of a girl barely in her twenties snuffed out by a drunken truck driver? Why? Why have you brought me here at Christmas?" All I can do is drop to my knees and cry.

Then the Holy Spirit began speaking to me.

"Look up. What do you see?"

A sharp cold wind cut across the cemetery, rustling the oak trees, as I obeyed His voice. From where I stood my eyes looked out over the nearby road.

"I see cars," was all I could answer."

"And what are they doing?"

"I don't know, going about their daily business, I guess."

His voice was gentler now. "That's right. They are shopping for holiday presents, picking up kids from school, going to and from work. Not one of them is thinking about this cemetery. Now, look around you and tell me what you see."

As I obeyed His voice again, I looked around and saw that I stood in the midst of a field of tombstones. Choking back tears, I murmured, "Dead people."

Once again He spoke to my heart. "That's right. You see the discarded remains of what their spirits have forever left behind. There isn't a single grave here that cares about its finances, its busy schedule, its Christmas shopping. Granite never cries. Every grave stone you see stands for only one thing—someone in Heaven or someone in hell."

"I know."

And then His voice wrapped itself around my heart and spoke these words. "What are you going to do about it? How are you going to spend the rest of your life? Will you live it to make a difference between who goes to Heaven and who goes to hell? Will you surrender your life to Me?"

As I reflected on His questions, He spoke to me one more time, then His presence lifted. "I want an answer before you drive out the gates of this cemetery. Regardless of your answer, I will ask you only once."

I walked back to my car, crawled into its warmth and slumped over my steering wheel. Sobbing, I took a deep breath, looked back across the landscape and replied, "You know the answer. I totally submit my life to Your will."

I drove out of the gates of death.

I know with great certainty that there is nothing unique about me.

If you are reading this book, it is because He is asking you the same questions He asked me. "How are you going to spend the rest of your life? Will you pursue the temporal or the eternal? Will your life's treasure be a small gray stone with numbers scratched into it or an eternal mansion in Heaven?"

All too soon we reach a point in our lives when we realize how fleeting the days are. And, deep down we know that if our pursuit consists solely of what is earthly and temporal we will come to the end of our days echoing Solomon's lament—"meaningless."

Simply put, we are here to prepare for abiding in eternity with our Creator and Lord. In an instant, our spirits will be pulled from our bodies. Those who are saved will be flooded from within with the glorious pure light of neverending worship and praise in the presence of the Lord. We must passionately pursue that day, knowing, "Now we see but a poor reflection as in a mirror; then we shall see face to face" (1 Cor. 13:12).

At the end of our struggles, turmoil, and persecution, waits a loving Savior who will lift us from our knees, wipe away our tears, and put a crown on our heads. As the reality of an eternal Heaven fully encompasses us, we will take that crown off and lay it at the feet of Jesus, able to say,

I have fought the good fight, I have finished the race, I have kept the faith.

2 Timothy 4:7

I have brought You glory on earth by completing the work You gave Me to do.

John 17:4

EPILOGUE

Do You Know Jesus?

My heartfelt desire is that this book has moved you toward a closer relationship with the Lord and a passionate seeking of His will for your life. The first step to knowing Him must be accepting the work of the cross. If you do not know Jesus as your personal Lord and Savior, please pray this prayer:

Lord Jesus, I am a sinner in need of a Savior. I believe that You are the Son of God and that You died on the cross, a living sacrifice for my sins. I surrender my life to You. Please forgive me for my sins, and create in me a new heart that desires to serve You all the days of my life. I accept You as my Lord and Savior. Amen.

If you have just prayed this prayer, you now need to do three things:

1. Find a Holy Spirit-filled church that teaches the Bible as the inerrant word of God and plant yourself in that church.

2. Buy a Bible and begin to read in it every day. I recommend an easy to understand translation. I also recommend that you begin reading in the New Testament in the Book of Matthew.

3. Pray daily. Your prayer does not need to be "fancy," but just a simple and heartfelt conversation between you and your Creator.

APPENDIX

Selected Biblical References to Treasures in Heaven

The following is a partial list of specific Scriptures that refer to treasures in Heaven:

Old Testament

He repays a man for what he has done; he brings upon him what his conduct deserves.

Job 34:11

One thing God has spoken, two things have I heard: that You, O God, are strong, and that You, O Lord, are loving. Surely You will reward each person according to what he has done.

Psalm 62:11-12

For God will bring every deed into judgment, including every hidden thing, whether it is good or evil.

Ecclesiastes 12:14

The Lord has made proclamation to the ends of the earth: "Say to the Daughter of Zion, 'See, your Savior comes! See, His reward is with Him, and His recompense accompanies Him'."

Isaiah 62:11

I the Lord search the heart and examine the mind, to reward a man according to his conduct, according to what his deeds deserve.

Jeremiah 17:10

The soul who sins is the one who will die. The son will not share the guilt of the father, nor will the father share the guilt of the son. The righteousness of the righteous man will be credited to him, and the wickedness of the wicked will be charged against him.

Ezekiel 18:20

This is what the Lord Almighty says: "If you will walk in My ways and keep My requirements, then you will govern My house and have charge of My courts, and I will give you a place among these standing here."

Zechariah 3:7

New Testament

Do not store up for yourselves treasures on earth, where moth and rust destroy, and where thieves break in and steal. But store up for yourselves treasures in heaven, where moth and rust do not destroy, and where thieves do not break in and steal. For where your treasure is, there your heart will be also.

Matthew 6:19-21

But small is the gate and narrow the road that leads to life, and only a few find it.

Matthew 7:14

Not everyone who says to Me, "Lord, Lord," will enter the kingdom of heaven, but only he who does the will of My Father who is in heaven.

Matthew 7:20

He who receives you receives Me, and he who receives Me receives the one who sent Me. Anyone who receives a prophet because he is a prophet will receive a prophet's reward, and anyone who receives a righteous man because he is a righteous man will receive a righteous man's reward. And if anyone gives even a cup of cold water to one of these little ones because he is My disciple, I tell you the truth, he will certainly not lose his reward.

Matthew 10:40

The one who received the seed that fell among the thorns is the man who hears the word, but the worries of this life and the deceitfulness of wealth choke it, making it unfruitful.

Matthew 13:22

For the Son of Man is going to come in His Father's glory with His angels, and then He will reward each person according to what he has done.

Matthew 16:27

And everyone who has left houses or brothers or sisters or father or mother or children or fields for My sake will receive a hundred times as much and will inherit eternal life. But many who are first will be last, and many who are last will be first.

Matthew 19:29-30

It will be good for that servant whose master finds him doing so when he returns. I tell you the truth, he will put him in charge of all his possessions.

Matthew 24:46-47

After a long time the master of those servants returned and settled accounts with them. The man who had received the five talents brought the other five. "Master," he said, "you entrusted me with five talents. See, I have gained five more."

His master replied, "Well done, good and faithful servant! You have been faithful with a few things; I will put you in charge of many things. Come and share your master's happiness!"

Matthew 25:19-21

Then the King will say to those on His right, "Come you who are blessed by my Father; take your inheritance, the kingdom prepared for you since the creation of the world. For I was hungry and you gave Me something to eat, I was thirsty and you gave Me something to drink, I was a stranger and you invited Me in, I needed clothes and you clothed Me, I was sick and you looked after Me, I was in prison and you came to visit Me."

Matthew 25:34-36

"I tell you the truth," Jesus replied, "no one who has left home or brothers or sisters or mother or father or children or fields for Me and the gospel will fail to receive a hundred times as much in this present age (homes, brothers, sisters, mothers, children and fields—and with them, persecutions) and in the age to come, eternal life. But many who are first will be last, and the last first."

Mark 10:29-31

Blessed are you when men hate you, when they exclude you and insult you and reject your name as evil, because of the Son of Man. Rejoice in that day and leap for joy, because great is your reward in heaven. For that is how their fathers treated the prophets.

Luke 6:22-23

Sell your possessions and give to the poor. Provide purses for yourselves that will not wear out, a treasure in heaven that will not be exhausted, where no thief comes near and no moth destroys.

Luke 12:33

I tell you, use worldly wealth to gain friends for yourselves, so that when it is gone, you will be welcomed into eternal dwellings.

Luke 16:9

When Jesus heard this, He said to him, "You still lack one thing. Sell everything you have and give to the poor, and you will have treasure in heaven. Then come, follow Me."

Luke 18:22

Do not work for food that spoils, but for food that endures to eternal life, which the Son of Man will give you.

John 6:27

For we will all stand before God's judgment seat. It is written: " 'As surely as I live,' says the Lord, 'every knee will bow before Me; every tongue will confess to God.' " So then each of us will give an account of himself to God.

Romans 14:10-12

The man who plants and the man who waters have one purpose, and each will be rewarded according to his own labor.

1 Corinthians 3:8

If any man builds on this foundation using gold, silver, costly stones, wood, hay or straw, his work will be shown for what it is, because the Day will bring it to light. It will be revealed with fire, and the fire will test the quality of each man's work. If what he has built survives, he will receive his reward. If it is burned up, he will suffer loss; he himself will be saved, but only as one escaping through the flames.

1 Corinthians 3:12-15

Therefore judge nothing before the appointed time; wait till the Lord comes. He will bring to light what is hidden in darkness and will expose the motives of men's hearts. At that time each will receive his praise from God.

1 Corinthians 4:5

For we must all appear before the judgment seat of Christ, that each one may receive what is due him for the things done while in the body, whether good or bad.

2 Corinthians 5:10

Do not be deceived: God cannot be mocked. A man reaps what he sows. The one who sows to please his sinful nature, from that nature will reap destruction; the one who sows to please the Spirit, from the Spirit will reap eternal life. Let us not become weary in doing good, for at the proper time we will reap a harvest if we do not give up. Therefore, as we have opportunity, let us do good to all people, especially to those who belong to the family of believers.

Galatians 6:7-10

For it is by grace you have been saved, through faith—and this not from yourselves, it is the gift of God—not by works, so that no one can boast. For we are God's workmanship, created in Christ Jesus to do good works, which God prepared in advance for us to do.

Ephesians 2:8-10

Serve wholeheartedly, as if you were serving the Lord, not men, because you know that the Lord will reward everyone for whatever good he does, whether he is slave or free.

Ephesians 6:7-8

Not that I have already obtained all this, or have already been made perfect, but I press on to take hold of that for which Christ Jesus took hold of me. Brothers, I do not consider myself yet to have taken hold of it. But one thing I do: Forgetting what is behind and straining toward what is ahead, I press on toward the goal to win the prize for which God has called me heavenward in Christ Jesus.

Philippians 3:12-14

Whatever you do, work at it with all your heart, as working for the Lord, not for men, since you know that you will receive an inheritance from the Lord as a reward. It is the Lord Christ you are serving. Anyone who does wrong will be repaid for his wrong, and there is no favoritism.

Colossians 3:23-25

Command them to do good, to be rich in good deeds, and to be generous and willing to share. In this way they will lay up treasure for themselves as a firm foundation for the coming age, so that they may take hold of the life that is truly life.

1 Timothy 6:18-19

I have fought the good fight, I have finished the race, I have kept the faith. Now there is in store for me the crown of righteousness, which the Lord, the righteous Judge, will award to me on that day—and not only to me, but also to all who have longed for His appearing.

2 Timothy 4:7-8

He regarded disgrace for the sake of Christ as of greater value than the treasures of Egypt, because he was looking ahead to his reward.

Hebrews 11:26

As the body without the spirit is dead, so faith without deeds is dead.

James 2:26

Praise be to the God and Father of our Lord Jesus Christ! In His great mercy He has given us new birth into a living hope through the resurrection of Jesus Christ from the dead, and into an inheritance that can never perish, spoil or fade—kept in heaven for you.

1 Peter 1:3-4

And when the Chief Shepherd appears, you will receive the crown of glory that will never fade away.

1 Peter 5:4

For this very reason, make every effort to add to your faith goodness; and to goodness, knowledge; and to knowledge, self-control; and to self-control, perseverance; and to perseverance, godliness; and to godliness brotherly kindness; and to brotherly kindness, love. For if you possess these qualities in increasing measure, they will keep you from being ineffective and unproductive in your knowledge of our Lord Jesus Christ....For if you do these things, you will never fall, and you will receive a rich welcome into the eternal kingdom of our Lord and Savior Jesus Christ.

2 Peter 1:5-8, 10-11

Do not love the world or anything in the world. If anyone loves the world, the love of the Father is not in him. For everything in the world—the cravings of sinful man, the lust of his eyes and the boasting of what he has and does—come not from the Father but from the world. The world and its desires pass away, but the man who does the will of God lives forever.

1 John 2:15-17

He who has an ear, let him hear what the Spirit says to the churches. To him who overcomes, I will give the right to eat from the tree of life, which is in the paradise of God.

Revelation 2:7

He who has an ear, let him hear what the Spirit says to the churches. He who overcomes will not be hurt at all by the second death.

Revelation 2:11

He who has an ear, let him hear what the Spirit says to the churches. To him who overcomes, I will give some of the hidden manna. I will also give him a white stone with a new name written on it, known only to him who receives it.

Revelation 2:17

Then all the churches will know that I am He who searches hearts and minds, and I will repay each of you according to your deeds.

Revelation 2:23b

To him who overcomes and does My will to the end, I will give authority over the nations—"He will rule them with an iron scepter; he will dash them to pieces like pottery"—just as I have received authority from My Father. I will also give him the morning star. He who has an ear, let him hear what the Spirit says to the churches.

Revelation 2:26-29

He who overcomes will, like them, be dressed in white. I will never blot out his name from the book of life, but will acknowledge his name before My Father and His angels. He who has an ear, let him hear what the Spirit says to the churches.

Revelation 3:5-6

I am coming soon. Hold on to what you have, so that no one will take your crown. Him who overcomes I will make a pillar in the temple of My God. Never again will he leave it. I will write on him the name of My God and the name of the city of My God, the new Jerusalem, which is coming down out of heaven from My God; and I will also write on him My new name. He who has an ear, let him hear what the Spirit says to the churches.

Revelation 3:11-13

To him who overcomes, I will give the right to sit with Me on my throne, just as I overcame and sat down with My Father on His throne. He who has an ear, let him hear what the Spirit says to the churches.

Revelation 3:21-22

Behold, I am coming soon! My reward is with Me, and I will give to everyone according to what he has done.

Revelation 20:12

ENDNOTES

1. Rick Joyner, *The Vision* (Nashville, TN: Thomas Nelson, Inc., 2000), p. 110.

2. Benny Hinn, *Good Morning, Holy Spirit* (Nashville, TN: Thomas Nelson Publishers, 1990), pp. 51-52.

You may contact Robert Katz at:

Katz, Gallagher & Company (APAC)
1515 Poydras Street, Suite 1800
New Orleans, Louisiana 70112

504-525-8524

rwkatz@katzgallagher.com

Other titles by Robert Katz, CPA *Money Came by the House the Other Day*. This is a complete guide to Christian Financial Planning and Stewardship, topics covered include: organizing your personal finances, debt management, stocks, bonds, buying a house, buying insurance, education expense, retirement planning, and much more.

To order call 1-800-622-4127 or email an order to

rwkatz@katzgallagher.com

Additional copies of this book and other
book titles from DESTINY IMAGE are
available at your local bookstore.

For a bookstore near you, call 1-800-722-6774

Send a request for a catalog to:

Destiny Image® Publishers, Inc.
P.O. Box 310
Shippensburg, PA 17257-0310

*"Speaking to the Purposes of God for This
Generation and for the Generations to Come"*

**For a complete list of our titles,
visit us at www.destinyimage.com**